FREE Test Taking Tips DVD Offer

To help us better serve you, we have developed a Test Taking Tips DVD that we would like to give you for <u>FREE</u>. **This DVD covers world-class test taking tips that you can use to be even more successful when you are taking your test.**

All that we ask is that you email us your feedback about your study guide. Please let us know what you thought about it – whether that is good, bad or indifferent.

To get your **FREE Test Taking Tips DVD**, email <u>freedvd@studyguideteam.com</u> with "FREE Test Taking Tips DVD" in the subject line and the following information in the body of the email:

    a.   The title of your study guide.

    b.   Your product rating on a scale of 1-5, with 5 being the highest rating.

    c.   Your feedback about the study guide. What did you think of it?

    d.   Your full name and shipping address to send your free DVD.

If you have any questions or concerns, please don't hesitate to contact us at <u>freedvd@studyguideteam.com</u>.

Thanks again!

AP Comparative Government & Politics Study Guide 2016

Table of Contents

Quick Overview

As you draw closer to taking your exam, preparing becomes more and more important. Thankfully, you have this study guide to help you get ready. Use this guide to help keep your studying on track and refer to it often.

This study guide contains several key sections that will help you be successful on your exam. The guide contains tips for what you should do the night before and the day of the test. Also included are test-taking tips. Knowing the right information is not always enough. Many well-prepared test takers struggle with exams. These tips will help equip you to accurately read, assess, and answer test questions.

A large part of the guide is devoted to showing you what content to expect on the exam and to helping you better understand that content. Near the end of this guide is a practice test so that you can see how well you have grasped the content. Then, answers explanations are provided so that you can understand why you missed certain questions.

Don't try to cram the night before you take your exam. This is not a wise strategy for a few reasons. First, your retention of the information will be low. Your time would be better used by reviewing information you already know rather than trying to learn lots of new information. Second, you will likely become stressed as you try to gain large amount of knowledge in a short amount of time. Third, you will be depriving yourself of sleep. So be sure to go to bed at a reasonable time the night before. Being well-rested helps you focus and remain calm.

Be sure to eat a substantial breakfast the morning of the exam. If you are taking the exam in the afternoon, be sure to have a good lunch as well. Being hungry is distracting and can make it difficult to focus. You have hopefully spent lots of time preparing for the exam. Don't let an empty stomach get in the way of success!

When travelling to the testing center, leave earlier than needed. That way, you have a buffer in case you experience any delays. This will help you remain calm and will keep you from missing your appointment time at the testing center.

Be sure to pace yourself during the exam. Don't try to rush through the exam. There is no need to risk performing poorly on the exam just so you can leave the testing center early. Allow yourself to use all of the allotted time if needed.

Remain positive while taking the exam even if you feel like you are performing poorly. Thinking about the content you should have mastered will not help you perform better on the exam. Once the exam is complete, take some time to relax. Even if you feel that you need to take the exam again, you will be well served by some down time before you begin studying again. It's often easier to convince yourself to study if you know that it will come with a reward!

Test-Taking Strategies

1. Predicting the Answer

When you feel confident in your preparation for a multiple-choice test, try predicting the answer before reading the answer choices. This is especially useful on questions that test objective factual knowledge or that ask you to fill in a blank. By predicting the answer before reading the available choices, you eliminate the possibility that you will be distracted or led astray by an incorrect answer choice. You will feel much more confident in your selection if you read the question, predict the answer, and then find your prediction among the answer choices. After using this strategy, be sure to still read all of the answer choices carefully and completely. If you feel unprepared, you should not attempt to predict the answers. This would be a waste of time and an opportunity for your mind to wander in the wrong direction.

2. Reading the Whole Question

Too often, test takers scan a multiple-choice question, recognize a few familiar words, and immediately jump to the answer choices. Test authors are aware of this common impatience, and they will sometimes prey upon it. For instance, a test author might subtly turn the question into a negative, or he or she might redirect the focus of the question right at the end. The only way to avoid falling into these traps is to read the entirety of the question carefully before reading the answer choices.

3. Looking for Wrong Answers

Long and complicated multiple-choice questions can be intimidating. One way to simplify a difficult multiple-choice question is to eliminate all of the answer choices that are clearly wrong. In most sets of answers, there will be at least one selection that can be dismissed right away. If the test is administered on paper, the test taker could draw a line through it to indicate that it may be ignored; otherwise, the test taker will have to perform this operation mentally or on scratch paper. In either case, once the obviously incorrect answers have been eliminated, the remaining choices may be considered. Sometimes identifying the clearly wrong answers will give the test taker some information about the correct answer. For instance, if one of the remaining answer choices is a direct opposite of one of the eliminated answer choices, it may well be the correct answer. The opposite of obviously wrong is obviously right! Of course, this is not always the case. Some answers are obviously incorrect simply because they are irrelevant to the question being asked. Still, identifying and eliminating some incorrect answer choices is a good way to simplify a multiple-choice question.

4. Don't Overanalyze

Anxious test takers often overanalyze questions. When you are nervous, your brain will often run wild causing you to make associations and discover clues that don't actually exist. If you feel that this may be a problem for you, do whatever you can to slow down during the test. Try taking a deep breath or counting to ten. As you read and consider the question, restrict yourself to the particular words used by the author. Avoid thought tangents about what the author *really* meant, or what he or she was *trying* to say. The only things that matter on a multiple-choice test are the words that are actually in the question. You must avoid reading too much into a multiple-choice question, or supposing that the writer meant something other than what he or she wrote.

5. No Need for Panic

It is wise to learn as many strategies as possible before taking a multiple-choice test, but it is likely that you will come across a few questions for which you simply don't know the answer. In this situation, avoid panicking. Because most multiple-choice tests include dozens of questions, the relative value of a single wrong answer is small. Moreover, your failure on one question has no effect on your success elsewhere on the test. As much as possible, you should compartmentalize each question on a multiple-choice test. In other words, you should not allow your feelings about one question to affect your success on the others. When you find a question that you either don't understand or don't know how to answer, just take a deep breath and do your best. Read the entire question slowly and carefully. Try rephrasing the question a couple of different ways. Then, read all of the answer choices carefully. After eliminating obviously wrong answers, make a selection and move on to the next question.

6. Confusing Answer Choices

When working on a difficult multiple-choice question, there may be a tendency to focus on the answer choices that are the easiest to understand. Many people, whether consciously or not, gravitate to the answer choices that require the least concentration, knowledge, and memory. This is a mistake. When you come across an answer choice that is confusing, you need to give it extra attention. A question might be confusing because you do not know the subject matter to which it refers. If this is the case, don't eliminate the answer before you have affirmatively settled on another. When you come across an answer choice of this type, set it aside as you look at the remaining choices. If you can confidently assert that one of the other choices is correct, you can leave the confusing answer aside. Otherwise, you will need to take a moment to try to better understand the confusing answer choice. Rephrasing is one way to tease out the sense of a confusing answer choice.

7. Your First Instinct

Many people struggle with multiple-choice tests because they overthink the questions. If you have studied sufficiently for the test, you should be prepared to trust your first instinct once you have carefully and completely read the question and all of the answer choices. There is a great deal of research to suggest that the mind can come to the correct conclusion very quickly once it has obtained all of the relevant information. At times, it may seem to you as if your intuition is working faster even than your reasoning mind. This may in fact be true. The knowledge you obtain while studying may be retrieved from your subconscious before you have a chance to work out the associations that support it. Verify your instinct by working out the reasons that it should be trusted.

8. Key Words

Many test takers struggle with multiple-choice questions because they have poor reading comprehension skills. Quickly reading and understanding a multiple-choice question requires a mixture of skill and experience. To help with this, try jotting down a few key words and phrases on a piece of scrap paper. Doing this concentrates the process of reading and forces the mind to weigh the relative importance of the question's parts. In selecting words and phrases to write down, the test taker thinks about the question more deeply and carefully. This is especially true for multiple-choice questions that are preceded by a long prompt.

9. Subtle Negatives

One of the oldest tricks in the multiple-choice test writer's book is to subtly reverse the meaning of a question with a word like *not* or *except*. If you are not paying attention to each word in the question, you can easily be led astray by this trick. For instance, a common question format is, "Which of the following is…?" Obviously, if the question instead is, "Which of the following is not….?," then the answer will be quite different. Even worse, the test makers are aware of the potential for this mistake and will include one answer choice that would be correct if the question were not negated or reversed. A test taker who misses the reversal will find what he or she believes to be a correct answer and will be so confident that he or she will fail to reread the question and discover the original error. The only way to avoid this is to practice a wide variety of multiple-choice questions and to pay close attention to each and every word.

10. Reading Every Answer Choice

It may seem obvious, but you should always read every one of the answer choices! Too many test takers fall into the habit of scanning the question and assuming that they understand the question because they recognize a few key words. From there, they pick the first answer choice that answers the question they believe they have read. Test takers who read all of the answer choices might discover that one of the latter answer choices is actually *more* correct. Moreover, reading all of the answer choices can remind you of facts related to the question that can help you arrive at the correct answer. Sometimes, a misstatement or incorrect detail in one of the latter answer choices will trigger your memory of the subject and will enable you to find the right answer. Failing to read all of the answer choices is like not reading all of the items on a restaurant menu. You might miss out on the perfect choice.

11. Spot the Hedges

One of the keys to success on multiple-choice tests is paying close attention to every word. This is never more true than with words like *almost*, *most*, *some*, and *sometimes*. These words are called "hedges", because they indicate that a statement is not totally true or not true in every place and time. An absolute statement will contain no hedges, but in many subjects, like literature and history, the answers are not always straightforward. There are always exceptions to the rules in these subjects. For this reason, you should favor those multiple-choice questions that contain hedging language. The presence of qualifying words indicates that the author is taking special care with his or her words, which is certainly important when composing the right answer. After all, there are many ways to be wrong, but there is only one way to be right! For this reason, it is wise when taking a multiple-choice test to avoid answers that are absolute. An absolute answer is one that says things are either all one way or all another. They often include words like *every*, *always*, *best*, and *never*. If you are taking a multiple-choice test in a subject that doesn't lend itself to absolute answers, be on your guard if you see any of these words.

12. Long Answers

In many subject areas, the answers are not simple. As already mentioned, the right answer often requires hedges. Another common feature of the answers to a complex or subjective question are qualifying clauses, which are groups of words that subtly modify the meaning of the sentence. If the question or answer choice describes a rule to which there are exceptions or the subject matter is complicated, ambiguous, or confusing, the correct answer will require many words in order to be expressed clearly and accurately. In essence, you should not be deterred by answer choices that seem excessively long. Oftentimes, the author of the text will not be able to write the correct answer without offering some qualifications and modifications. As a test taker, your job is to read the answer choices thoroughly and completely and to select the one that most accurately and precisely answers the question.

13. Restating to Understand

Sometimes, a question on a multiple-choice test is difficult not because of what it asks but because of how it is written. If this is the case, restate the question or answer choice in different words. This process serves a couple of important purposes. First, it forces you to concentrate on the core of the question. In order to rephrase the question accurately, you have to understand it well. Rephrasing the question will concentrate your mind on the key words and ideas. Second, it will present the information to your mind in a fresh way. This process may trigger your memory of some useful scrap of information picked up while studying.

14. True Statements

Sometimes an answer choice will be true in itself, but it does not answer the question. This is one of the main reasons why it is essential to read the question carefully and completely before proceeding to the answer choices. Too often, test takers skip ahead to the answer choices and look for true statements. Having found one of these, they are content to select it without reference to the question above. Obviously, this provides an easy way for test makers to play tricks. The savvy test taker will always read the entire question before turning to the answer choices. Then, having settled on a correct answer choice, he or she will refer to the original question and ensure that the selected answer is relevant. The mistake of choosing a correct-but-irrelevant answer choice is especially common on questions related to specific pieces of objective knowledge, like historical or scientific facts. A prepared test taker will have a wealth of factual knowledge at his or her disposal, but may be careless in its application.

15. No Patterns

One of the more dangerous ideas that circulate about multiple-choice tests is that the correct answers tend to fall into patterns. These erroneous ideas range from a belief that B and C are the most common right answers, to the idea that an unprepared test-taker should answer "A-B-A-C-A-D-A-B-A." It cannot be emphasized enough that pattern-seeking of this type is exactly the WRONG way to approach a multiple-choice test. To begin with, it is highly unlikely that the test maker will plot the correct answers according to some predetermined pattern. The questions are scrambled and delivered in a random order. Furthermore, even if the test maker was following a pattern in the assignation of correct answers, there is no reason why the test maker would know which pattern he or she was using. Any attempt to discern a pattern in the answer choices is a waste of time and a distraction from the real work of taking the test. A test taker would be much better served by extra preparation before the test than by reliance on a pattern in the answers.

Introduction to Comparative Politics

Comparative politics

Comparativists, or those who study comparative politics, place the political events of the present in a historical context. In general, these academics are concerned with creating overarching political theories that can be applied to all sorts of situations. To this end, they focus on governmental structure and its effects on the behavior of a nation and its citizenry. Comparative political scientists are especially concerned with the development and evolution of nations over time.

Normative and empirical questions

Comparativists must grapple with normative questions, which deal with the ethical value of political actions, and empirical questions, which concern matters of fact. In some sense, a normative question can only be answered with an opinion. For this reason, many political scientists eschew this sort of question. For example, comparative political scientists may avoid questions related to the morality of certain systems of government or certain political actions. Comparative political scientists are more likely to attend to empirical questions, which can be settled through investigation. For instance, a political scientist might try to determine the effects of different geographies or political structures on the development of a nation because many aspects of these topics can be explored through research and statistical analysis.

Scope and methods of study among comparativists

Comparativist political scientists are usually affiliated with one of three main approaches: rational choice comparativism, structuralism, and culturalism. A rational choice comparativist uses mathematics and statistics to explore politics and government. The work of a rational choice comparativist is similar to that of an economist. A structuralist, on the other hand, looks for similarities in political behavior in different contexts, with the aim of constructing broad, overarching theories. A structuralist seeks to advance theories that can be applied to many different nations. Finally, a culturalist emphasizes the details on the ground. These academics visit and often live among the people they are studying. They amass a great deal of data, which they are often reticent to apply outside of the specific context in which it was obtained.

Cultural approach
Culturalist political scientists operate much like anthropologists; that is, they perform research on the ground and limit the application of their findings to the specific group they are studying. Culturalists pay particular attention to the political and cultural orientation of villages and small groups. They view culture

as a lens through which to view politics. The only theories produced by culturalists are those having to do with the particular group being studied. During the 1980s and 1990s, academia moved away from the culturalist approach, favoring instead the pseudo-mathematical precision of the structuralists. Another reason for the decline of the culturalist approach is the expense associated with long research trips; governments and universities have become less willing to fund these sorts of ventures.

Structural and rational choice approaches
Structuralist political scientists gather information about government, political parties, and social strata, and they use this information to construct broad theories about human political behavior. As much as possible, structuralists try to rely on data gathered in the field; however, some of this data can be difficult to trust. Rational choice political scientists, on the other hand, rely almost exclusively on mathematics, statistics, and game theory. These academics are also interested in universally applicable theories, but they rely solely on data and exclude anecdotal information.

Theory of decisions

In comparative government, the theory of decisions is the idea that personal political choices are influenced both by the beliefs and experiences of the decision maker and by the information provided to him. To some extent, the actors in a political system are dependent on the quality of information they receive. However, the members of a polity are likely to make vastly different decisions based on the same information. Comparative political scientists try to isolate those personal and environmental factors that exercise significant influence on political decisions.

Dependency theory

According to dependency theory, financial and natural resources naturally shift from poorly developed countries to industrialized countries. In other words, this theory asserts that rich states will tend to become richer, and poor states will tend to become poorer. Before this theory was advanced, many political scientists had believed that all states have a tendency toward industrialization and that the differences between states are simply due to varying degrees of progress along this path. However, dependency theory suggests that underdeveloped countries may never become developed if they are not given special assistance. Indeed, those who support this theory assert that today's underdeveloped countries are relatively less developed than any of today's industrialized countries ever were. Wealthy countries exploit the cheap labor and resources of underdeveloped nations, thereby perpetuating underdevelopment.

Inference

An inference is a conclusion based on an established set of information. While an inference is not itself a fact, it should be based on facts. A deductive inference proceeds from general statements to a specific conclusion. The following is a classic example of deductive reasoning: "All men are mortal. Socrates is a man. Therefore, Socrates is mortal." Inductive reasoning, by contrast, proceeds from specific examples to general ideas. The following is an example of inductive reasoning: "Socrates is a man. Socrates is mortal. Therefore, all men are mortal." In political science, and especially in comparative political research, inferences are needed to make conclusions about political behavior. Some comparative political scientists focus on granular, on-the-ground research, which they use to create general theories. Other comparativists create general theories in the opposite direction by moving from general principles to specific applications.

Common policy challenges

Governments strive to meet the needs and desires of the people, but they are often restrained by cost. There are often disagreements between rival factions over the proper course of legislation. To pay for necessary services, a government may need to raise taxes, which will not be appreciated by the public. In the modern world, governments are mainly preoccupied with issues like the environment, health care, infrastructure, the economy, education, and foreign relations.

Important terms

- State: any country that has an established border, a fixed population, and its own organized government
- Nation: a state whose citizens share a language, a culture, and—often—a religion
- Regime: a particular iteration of government in a nation, usually headed by a charismatic leader. For example, Iraqis suffered for many years during the Saddam Hussein regime.
- Government: an organized institution responsible for making and enforcing laws in a particular area and for a particular people
- Politics: the set of behaviors and activities that relate to the operation of government
- Political science: the academic discipline concerned with the structure and operation of government

Sovereignty, Authority, and Power

Political culture

Political culture is the beliefs and values that are generally held by the members of a political group. The political culture of a group includes its organization, that is, whether it is democratic or led by a strong single power. Some of the most widely known political cultures are socialism, democracy, fascism, anarchism, and oligarchy:

- Anarchism: a condition in which there is no government authority. When anarchism has occurred in history, it has usually been among a group of relatives who share a very similar culture and set of beliefs.
- Oligarchy: government led by a small group of people. Oligarchies are notorious for existing primarily to advance the interests of the powerful few.
- Fascism: government led by a dictator and marked by devaluation of the individual and promotion of industry and the military
- Democracy: government in which decisions are made by the people, either directly or through elected representatives

Political communication

Political communication flows up and down, from the top-ranking officials in government to citizens as well as from the citizens up to government officials. The most intense period of political communication in a democracy is during election season when the public is making its demands known to candidates and candidates are simultaneously broadcasting their views to the public. Political communication has become so important that governments have special departments solely committed to handling radio licenses, press releases, and television broadcasts. Political communication can consist of campaign commercials, government literature, and speeches. Often, organizations with special interests will undertake a marketing campaign to promote a particular issue or law. The Internet has created all sorts of new ways for governments to communicate with citizens and vice versa.

Political socialization

The phrase political socialization is used to describe the process by which a person learns about and becomes active in politics. For most people, this process occurs during childhood, though it may occur at anytime of life. The primary agent of political socialization is the family, especially the parents. Children tend to adopt the political views of their parents, assuming their parents discuss political issues in the home. However, children are also influenced by the political views of their friends and classmates. Significant but lesser influences on political socialization include social class, religious beliefs, and media exposure.

Nation and state

In the field of comparative politics, there is a subtle difference between a nation and a state. A nation is defined as any group with a common language, religion, and culture. For instance, even within the United States, political scientists recognize distinct Native American nations. A state, meanwhile, is a whole country. This meaning of state is distinct from the word, as it is used in the sense of "United States," that denotes subdivisions of an entire country. There are four essential qualities for statehood: established boundaries, a permanent population, an organized government, and the ability of the government to assert authority over things like the economy and foreign relations.

Failed state

There is some dispute among political scientists over what constitutes a failed state, but most experts agree that a state has failed when it cannot conduct foreign policy, when it cannot provide services to its people, when its leader has no legal authority, or when it loses control over part of its territory. A major economic crisis usually accompanies these conditions and contributes to further failure. Some present-day states that are generally agreed to have failed are Nigeria, Afghanistan, Somalia, and Sudan.

Nigeria
In 1960, Great Britain granted Nigeria independence. However, the African nation's jubilation was quickly marred by power struggles between rival ethnic and religious groups. Nigeria began with a parliamentary government, but by 1966 this corrupt system had been overthrown by the military, led by Igbo tribesman Aguiyi Ironsi. There was an immediate and violent backlash against the Igbos, which led to their attempted secession in 1967. The resulting civil war did not end until Great Britain intervened in 1970. The Igbos ultimately did not secede. Nigeria's Second Republic, which was initiated in 1979 on the American model of constitutional democracy, quickly became rife with corruption and was replaced by military rule in 1983. The most recent attempt at civil government began in 1999, but the Nigerian nation continues to be beset by ethnic conflict.

First world, second world, and third world countries

In the middle of the twentieth century, as the United States vied with the Soviet Union for global hegemony, it was fashionable to divide the globe into first, second, and third world nations. A first world nation had developed industry and a basically democratic government. The United States, Great Britain, and Canada were all examples of first world nations. A second world nation, by contrast, had developed industry but had not yet attained democracy. The Soviet Union and its eastern European allies were all considered second world. Most nations, including those of Africa and the Caribbean, were considered to be third world because they had neither industry nor democracy.

Once known as the first world, nations like the United States, France, Great Britain, Japan, and Germany are now known as industrialized democracies, as liberal democracies, or as developed countries. Industrialized democracies have enabled a very high standard of living for their citizens and wield significant international power. Their governments vary in some details, but they generally promote individual rights and the protection of private property. The economy in an industrialized democracy is largely made up of service, industrial, and agricultural businesses. Meanwhile, those nations that were once designated as second world are now regularly called communist or post-communist. Although countries like Poland, the Czech Republic, and parts of the former Soviet Bloc are industrialized, they have not yet achieved a full democracy. Some other second world countries, like Cuba, North Korea, Vietnam, and China, are still avowedly communist. Economically, these countries are moving toward the free market, but they still place great restrictions on the rights of their citizens.

Those formerly third world countries that have made the greatest progress are called developing countries. Among these, the most successful are the newly industrialized countries, which include Mexico, Taiwan, South Korea, Singapore, South Africa, India, and many of the countries in South America. All these countries have stable if not democratic governments and vibrant manufacturing sectors. The less developed countries also were considered third world, but they have not yet made great progress. Countries like Colombia, Nigeria, and the Philippines are defined as less developed because they have shaky governments and rely on a narrow range of exports. Finally, the former third world countries that have developed political systems based on Islam are known as Islamic states. There are twenty-six such nations. Islamic states derive the structure of their governments and judicial systems from the Koran and the authority of religious leaders.

European Union

In 1957, the Treaty of Rome created a special coal and steel market, in which tariffs would be regulated, for West Germany, France, Italy, Luxembourg, Holland, and Belgium. By 1985, this market, known as the European Economic Community (EEC), would expand to include Sweden, Austria, Finland, Spain, Portugal, Greece, Denmark, Ireland, and Britain. The Maastricht treaty of 1991 established a single currency, known as the euro, which was adopted by all the members except Britain (which did not want to abandon the pound), Denmark, Greece (which did not qualify), and Sweden. In 2001, the Treaty of Nice allowed the entry of new members, and in 2004, ten formerly communist eastern European nations joined. These countries did not become full members, however, meaning they do not use the euro or have equal power within the organization.

Like many nations, the European Union has a parliament, though its members represent nations rather than political parties. Each of the twenty-seven member nations elects legislators to the EU Parliament. At present, the members of the EU Parliament are drawn from twelve different political parties. This body cannot create legislation; it can only approve or disapprove of it. For this reason, it is considered to be a weak institution. One of the major documents of the EU is the Charter of Fundamental Rights, which forbids capital punishment and mandates universal health care and equal pay for men and women. The most important element of the EU's judiciary is the Court of Justice, which is composed of one judge from each of the twenty-seven member nations. This body is charged with looking over all the laws passed and court decisions rendered by member nations.

In 2004, a proposed EU constitution achieved near-unanimous support, but the constitution ultimately failed because France and Holland disapproved. The nations went back to the drawing board and ultimately produced the Treaty of Lisbon. After being ratified by all the EU member nations, the document took effect in December 2009. (Ireland voted against the treaty at first but then voted for it.) The treaty created a rotating presidency system with six-month terms. The EU Parliament was given power over the European Commission and the Council of Ministers. However, the EU Parliament can only ratify or veto legislation; it cannot introduce it. Laws must be put forth by the European Commission and the Council of Ministers. These bodies are composed of the heads of state from each member country. Obviously, divergent national interests make cooperation and compromise necessary.

Associated terms:
- Convergence criteria: Before they are allowed to use the euro, EU member countries must meet standards for debt, deficit, and currency exchange rates. These standards are collectively known as the convergence criteria. As an example, in the 1990s, Greece was not permitted to adopt the euro because it did not meet the convergence criteria.
- Stability pact: mandates that each EU member country keep its budget deficit at less than 3 percent of its gross domestic product and maintain an annual inflation rate of 3 percent or less
- Common agricultural policy: mandates that farmers in all EU countries receive the same subsidies. One result of the common agricultural policy has been abnormally high prices for some products. For this reason, France and other countries have complained vociferously against this policy.

Political power

In political science, political power is simply the ability to make decisions in the government. Most of the time, powerful groups will have particular agendas that have been established by dominant leadership. The decisions made by these groups will tend to support their respective agendas. Political power is also evident in the ability to shape the preferences of the populace. In other words, the group that is in power can provide information that will lead most people to support the furtherance of that group's agenda. In a more idealistic light, political power belongs to the people, who consent to be governed based on the understanding that the leaders will act in the best interests of the people. This is how democracy is supposed to work; however, this ideal view is often compromised by the avarice of those who hold power.

Constitutions

A constitution is a document that explains how a country or state government will operate. Typically, a constitution begins with a preamble, which lays out the reasons for its composition. After this, most constitutions include a series of articles that detail the organization and procedures of the government. Some countries have constitutions but do not pay much attention to them. This is especially true when the constitution does not allow for a judiciary, which would determine whether government actions are constitutional. Some constitutions establish a state religion, but many are secular and do not affirm any particular religion as preeminent. A constitution may be used to establish any sort of government: socialist, democratic, or parliamentary, just to name a few.

People's Republic of China
In the People's Republic of China, the government operates according to a socialist constitution, which was ratified on December 4, 1982. This was the fourth iteration of the Chinese constitution. According to this document, China is a socialist republic, and all power lies with the people. There is actually a legislature in China, though it does no more than confirm decisions made in the upper reaches of the Communist Party. There is no judiciary in China, meaning there is no body that determines the constitutionality of government actions. A great deal of the Chinese constitution concerns the distinction between private property and government property. For instance, the government largely has control of the means of production, but some individuals are allowed to operate on their own. All the land in Chinese cities is the property of the government, and all the land in the country is owned by collectives. In other words, land may not be bought or sold by individuals.

Iran

The constitution of the Islamic Republic of Iran is overtly religious: the second article declares that the fundamental principles of government in the nation are divine justice, the afterlife, divine revelation, monotheism, the continuance of the Islamic revolution, and the intrinsic dignity and value of man. All the laws in Iran must be based on Islamic ideas. For example, the family must be the fundamental unit of Iranian society, and the members of the local councils and the Islamic Consultative Assembly must be freely elected. Although Islam is affirmed as the national religion, Iranians are allowed to practice Judaism, Zoroastrianism, and Christianity. The constitution of Iran also declares that non-Iranians will be respected and treated with care so long as they do not act against the interests of Iran or Islam.

Federal Republic of Nigeria

In 1999, the Nigerian government affirmed its new constitution without submitting it for public approval. The Nigerian constitution is largely based on that of the United States: it divides the government into legislative, judicial, and executive branches, and it establishes two legislative houses. It also enumerates the fundamental rights of Nigerians. The Nigerian constitution asserts that political parties must be national and must have their headquarters in the capital city of Abuja. To win the presidency, a candidate must receive a majority of the total votes and at least one-quarter of the votes in two-thirds of the states. The point of these restrictions is to avoid domination by one ethnic group, though one of the practical results is to encourage two-party politics. An odd omission in the constitution was highlighted in 2009, when President Alhaji Umaru Yar'Adua fell ill. The constitution had no protocol for succession, so Vice President Goodluck Jonathan did not have any authority when he took over. The legislature had to be assembled in a hurry to issue a special act allowing Jonathan to govern.

Mexico

When devising their constitution, Mexico's legislators were concerned about the possibility of a single ruler dominating the country for decades. For this reason, they forbade the president from serving more than one six-year term. Also, Mexican politicians are forbidden from seeking reelection to the same office. Despite these provisions in the constitution, Mexico was dominated by the PRI party for years. Mexican presidents exploited the system for their own gain. The Mexican constitution, which was drafted on February 5, 1917, arranges the government in much the same way as that of the United States. Article 123 outlines workers' rights, including the eight-hour workday, the right to strike, and a mandatory day of rest. Until this provision was ratified, Mexico had been the scene of rampant worker exploitation. As of 2005, capital punishment was outlawed in Mexico.

Post-communist Russian Federation
In 1993, Boris Yeltsin led the effort to draft and pass a constitution of the Russian Federation. This constitution established a government with a strong executive branch somewhat limited by a legislature and a judiciary as well as a system of checks and balances. However, whenever a national emergency was claimed, the president was allowed to seize control, dissolving the legislature and, if he desired, initiating national referenda or elections. It quickly became clear that even though this government was ostensibly ruled by the legislature, the executive could maneuver his way to a preeminent position rather easily.

Great Britain
Great Britain is an interesting model of a nation that remains stable despite not having a formal constitution. Britain does depend on King John's Magna Carta of 1215 and the Act of Settlement of 1701 (which describes the line of royal succession), but national affairs are governed in large part by case law and historical precedent. If a majority of both houses of Parliament approve, the "constitution" can be amended. This process is only complete, however, when the queen gives her royal assent. In general, the British system is founded on the supremacy of Parliament and the rule of law. In other words, Parliament is affirmed as the primary legislative body in the nation with the authority to determine the royal succession, control royal authority, and mandate term limits for its members.

Regimes

A regime is a type of government, or the duration of a particular government or leader's control in a country. Authoritarian regime is the organizational structure in which one person or a small group controls the political, educational, financial, economic, and diplomatic functions of the country. A totalitarian regime is a regime that is organized around a central idea. Perhaps the best example of a totalitarian regime is the National Socialist state that existed in Germany between 1936 and 1945. Adolf Hitler and the other leaders of this movement promoted the idea that Germans were a master race engaged in a battle to the death with other ethnic groups. In the Soviet Union, leaders like Lenin and Stalin based a totalitarian regime around the idea of class struggle. In a totalitarian regime, government control is pervasive, and it is difficult for citizens to obtain or disseminate information contrary to the interests of the regime. A democratic regime is a system in which citizens have the ability to vote directly on the issues or to elect leaders. Some of the varieties of democracy include presidential, parliamentary, and veto player.

Russia
Vladimir Ilyich Lenin founded the communist Soviet Union and was succeeded by Joseph Stalin. Stalin's totalitarian regime aimed to industrialize the country, in part by forcing the migration of peasants to the cities. Stalin stopped at nothing in pursuit of his plan. He murdered thousands of farmers who resisted forced

migration, and his program for turning over the countryside to collectives resulted in massive famines that killed millions. Stalin's so-called "Five-Year Plans" established unrealistic goals for industrial production and then imposed harsh living conditions on citizens in pursuit of these goals. Stalin died in 1953, with the blood of perhaps 20 million people on his hands. Stalin's successor, Nikita Khrushchev, repudiated him in 1956.

In 1985, Mikhail Gorbachev became general secretary of the Communist Party in the Soviet Union. Gorbachev had three goals: perestroika, or industrial reform; democratization; and glasnost, or openness to the rest of the world. None of these initiatives was wholly successful. His campaign for industrial reform was stymied by production managers who did not want to take responsibility. Meanwhile, his democratization efforts resulted in the election of candidates who were not members of the Communist Party. For instance, Boris Yeltsin, not a member of the Communist Party was elected president in 1991. Finally, the glasnost policy foundered because members of the news media were not allowed to criticize current leaders or policies, though they were permitted to criticize the leaders and policies of the past. Ultimately, Gorbachev was forced to resign, and on December 25, 1991, after surviving an attempted coup, he broke up the Union of Soviet Socialist Republics (USSR).

After the resignation of Gorbachev and the disbanding of the USSR, Boris Yeltsin took over as president of the Russian Federation. The constitution he delivered in 1993 placed a great deal of power with the executive, but it was approved by Russian voters. Some members of the Duma from the communist era conspired to overthrow Yeltsin, but he put down this nascent rebellion. Rather than gradually introduce a market economy, Yeltsin attempted "shock therapy," which caused hyperinflation at rates higher than 100 percent. Meanwhile, Moscow and St. Petersburg were overtaken by criminal gangs. In 1995, Russians elected very conservative and communist candidates, and in 1996, Yeltsin won reelection only because he was supported by a coalition of wealthy businessmen. His second term was marked by illness and miscalculations, leading to the crash of the ruble in 1998 and Yeltsin's ultimate resignation on December 31, 1999.

Yeltsin was replaced by his final prime minister, a former KGB official named Vladimir Putin. Putin would prove to be a strong leader, evidenced early on by his military invasion of Chechnya after a separatist group from that region was blamed for the bombing of a Moscow apartment building in 1999. This invasion played well with the Russian populace, and after the Unity Party, which backed Putin, dominated the elections of December 1999, Putin himself was elected president the following March. He was able to improve the Russian economy, but the Chechen War dragged on, and crime became a major problem in the cities. In the 2003 elections, control of the Duma was seized by the United Russia party, which supported Putin. At this point, Putin's rule became more autocratic: he took control of the media and intimidated many would-be challengers to his presidency. He won reelection in a rout in 2004. The Russian constitution forbade Putin from running again in 2008, but his handpicked successor, Dmitry Medvedev, won the election and immediately installed Putin as prime minister, where he continues to exercise a major influence.

People's Republic of China
In 1949, Mao Zedong began his twenty-seven-year reign as self-styled paramount leader. His major goal was to industrialize China, which at that time was a largely agrarian society. The Great Leap Forward, initiated in 1958, was an ambitious fifteen-year plan for modernization. It was a disaster, marked by crop shortages and starvation, and it was ultimately discontinued after only two years. Another communist program, the Cultural Revolution, lasted from 1966 to 1976. This was an attempt to inculcate communist values and eliminate any subversion. Youths, known as the Red Guard, were encouraged to turn in those they suspected of disloyalty. Those unlucky enough to be detained for subversion were beaten, sent to work camps for "reorientation," and often killed. At the same time, the Red Guard was tasked with destroying all the artifacts of pre-communist China, including buildings, artworks, and historic texts.

In 1976, Mao Zedong died, creating a power vacuum. After a struggle, Deng Xiaoping wrested control from Mao's widow, leader of the so-called "Gang of Four." After assuming the mantle of paramount leader, Deng initiated a program that loosely translates as "socialism with Chinese characteristics." This program focused on four areas of modernization: business, farming, education, and the military. Deng created special economic zones for foreign investment in large Chinese cities. At the same time, Deng's "mass line" approach motivated peasants to sell their surplus crops, and citizens were forbidden from having more than one child. One of the final events of the Deng period was the massacre of unarmed pro-democracy protesters in Tiananmen Square in 1989.

The programs of the Deng regime were for the most part continued by Jiang Zemin. The government was very concerned with preventing any future episodes like Tiananmen, so the Chinese justice system became even more oppressive. Moreover, Jiang continued the internal passport system, which prevented Chinese citizens from moving freely throughout the country. The Falun Gong, a group of religious dissidents, was harshly repressed, and Tibet was prevented from asserting independence. However, Jiang also promoted the Special Economic Zone program and worked to get China admitted to the World Trade Organization. He also enabled the campaign that brought the 2008 Summer Olympics to Beijing. Both Macao and Hong Kong rejoined China but were allowed to maintain their local governments, an arrangement known as "one country, two systems." Taiwan declined to enter China this way. In 2002, Jiang Zemin retired at the age of seventy-six.

Great Britain
Although Great Britain is nominally ruled by a monarch, the real power resides with Parliament. Great Britain does not have a written constitution; instead, it relies on historical precedent and case law. The country's legislature consists of a House of Lords and a House of Commons. Membership in the House of Lords is hereditary. This house can create bills, but it does not have very much power. The House of Lords serves as the highest court of appeals in Great Britain. The members of the House of Commons, on the other hand, are elected. This body is run by a prime minister, selected by the representatives of the majority party. In recent years, the New Labour Party and the Conservative Party have dominated British politics, though the Liberal Democrats have been gaining prominence. The leadership of the majority party has the responsibility for calling elections, though they must do so within five years of taking office.

When Margaret Thatcher became prime minister of Great Britain in 1979, she vowed to wrest control of the country from the union leaders who had gained so much power under Labour Party governments. She also strove to create a more muscular foreign policy, resulting in the Falklands crisis with Argentina in 1982. In 1984 and 1985, Thatcher suppressed striking coal miners, making good on her pledge to marginalize unions. At the same time, she turned several government-owned industries over to private concerns. Some of these businesses included British Steel, Rolls Royce, and British Petroleum. Thatcher discontinued the practice of subsidizing housing, and she sold all houses owned by the state. During her regime, taxes and inflation declined, but unemployment and homelessness grew. She became increasingly controversial, and in 1990, John Major was selected as prime minister by the Conservative Party.

John Major was relatively inexperienced when he became prime minister, a situation that was not helped by the almost immediate controversy over Britain's entry into the European Union. British people were especially opposed to the idea of adopting the euro and abandoning the pound. Major handled that issue by putting it to a public vote, but his administration continued to be bedeviled by minor scandals and crises like mad cow disease. Though it was perhaps not his fault, Major seems to have presided over the end of a Conservative era in British politics. He resigned in 1995, and the New Labour Party took control of Parliament in 1997.

In 1997, the New Labour Party took control of Parliament and installed Tony Blair as prime minister. Although his party was considered leftist, Blair was more moderate and indeed moved to have socialism removed from the New Labour Party's charter. Blair placed a premium on public opinion and called for referenda on all sorts of controversial issues, as for instance the relative independence of Northern Ireland, Wales, and Scotland. Blair also queried the British public on EU membership, adoption of the euro, and peace with Northern Ireland. During the Blair administration, Britain adopted a minimum wage law and further diminished the voting rights of the House of Lords. Although the New Labour Party retained control in 2007, Gordon Brown succeeded Blair as prime minister.

Mexico

Even though its 1917 constitution made room for multiple political parties in the federal system, Mexican politics was dominated by the Institutional Revolutionary Party (PRI) for seventy years. Furthermore, Mexican presidents wielded exceptional power. Although PRI candidates were in control from the 1920s to 2000, they changed their positions quite a bit over time. Indeed, the policy swings of PRI were part of a "pendulum theory" designed to maintain control of the government. Each PRI president would handpick his successor, a process known as "dedazo." Of course, PRI's control was aided by its domination of the news media, which allowed the party to control the information available to voters and repress any attempt at subversion.

Carlos Salinas became president of Mexico under a cloud of suspicion: the computer tallying election results had crashed right after displaying a slim lead for Democratic Party of the Revolution (PRD) candidate Cuauhtémoc Cardenas. After it had been repaired, the computer showed Salinas in the lead. Despite this dubious beginning, Salinas quickly earned domestic and international support by privatizing highway construction, airlines, mines, banks, and the telephone service, and by joining the United States and Canada in the North American Free Trade Agreement (NAFTA). Unfortunately, any economic progress was undone by a currency crash in 1993, and Salinas's popularity was further diminished by ongoing bloody conflict in Chiapas with a rebel peasant group known as the Zapatistas. Salinas had planned for Donald Luis Colosio to succeed him, but Colosio was assassinated in Tijuana in 1994. The blame for this murder and the killing of PRI's secretary general in Mexico City was pinned on Raul Salinas, the president's brother, who also was caught with a considerable amount of stolen money. Carlos Salinas was so unpopular at the end of his term as president that he had to flee to Ireland.

Ernesto Zedillo

Ernesto Zedillo became known as the "accidental president" of Mexico because he only became the PRI candidate after the murder of Donald Luis Colosio. As president, Zedillo borrowed extensively from the United States to shore up the Mexican economy. At the same time, he modernized PRI by empowering the "tecnicos" (technocrats) and diminishing the power of "los dinos," the party's old guard. Zedillo also improved the election process by allowing observers, installing computer vote counters, creating voter cards, and establishing an independent election authority known as IFE. Moreover, he broke the tradition of handpicking his successor, instead creating a primary system for PRI candidates. Although Zedillo can be praised for these actions, the short-term result was that PRI lost some of its stature in Mexico.

<u>Vicente Fox</u>
With the election of PAN party candidate Vicente Fox in 2000, Mexico had a president who was not a member of PRI for the first time since 1917. Fox had a background in business, as president of Coca-Cola's Mexican operation, and in government, as governor of the state of Guanajuato. He immediately tried to negotiate a better immigration policy with the United States, but these efforts were unfortunately derailed by the terrorist attacks of September 11, 2001. In the wake of 9/11, the United States was unwilling to cooperate on a deal that would admit more foreigners. At the same time, Fox struggled to reach legislative compromises with the PRI and PRD representatives, and he continued to be weighed down by the ongoing conflict in Chiapas. Though Fox was able to make some positive changes to the Mexican judiciary, his declining popularity was demonstrated by the primary defeat of his handpicked successor, Santiago Creel. In the end, though, Fox was succeeded by Felipe Calderon, another member of the PAN party.

<u>Nigeria</u>
Nigeria has endured a series of oppressive military regimes, not the least of which was led by Ibrahim Babangida. In 1985, Babangida took control of Nigeria and pledged to restore civilian rule after he had fixed the workings of the government. To do so, however, he claimed that it was necessary to move the capital to an ethnically mixed location, mandate a two-party-only system, take a new census, forbid current and former politicians from seeking office again, and create ethnically mixed states by redrawing boundaries. In a hopeful sign, Babangida called for local elections in 1992. However, when Moshood Abiola appeared to win the election, Babangida invalidated the results, claiming fraud. Violent riots ensued. The popular perception of Babangida was not improved by subsequent revelations that he had amassed an enormous fortune while in office.

Babangida's rule was tranquil compared to that of his successor, Sani Abacha. Abacha took over control of Nigeria in 1993 and immediately began a campaign of violence against his political adversaries. Abacha's victims included Moshood Abiola, who most analysts believe defeated Babangida in the 1992 election, and Abiola's wife. Former leader Olusegun Obasanjo was jailed on trumped-up charges and Nobel Prize-winning author Wole Soyinka was forced into exile. Indeed, the Abacha regime drove much of Nigeria's intelligentsia out, which had calamitous economic consequences. A particularly low moment was the execution of ten Ogonis, including the writer Ken Saro-Wiwa, who were protesting the destruction of farmland by oil companies, most notably Shell. Abacha's death in 1998 led to the creation of a new constitution known as the Fourth Republic. The freed Obasanjo took control of the Nigerian government in 1999 amid great hope, but he was unable to quell the tribal conflict.

Iran

In the present organization of Iran, the most powerful person is the religious leader known as the faqih. The faqih, at present Ali Hosseini-Khameini, has power over the military, the judiciary, and the media. Iran is a self-styled Islamic Republic with a unicameral legislature, whose 209 members serve four-year terms. Iran does not allow political parties, and most political power in Iran is vested in the Council of Guardians (which selects the candidates for parliament) and the Supreme Court. Since 2005, the president of Iran has been Mahmoud Ahmadinejad. During his term, the nation has moved forward on a nuclear program while attempting to diversify its oil-based economy. International observers considered Ahmadinejad's 2009 reelection to be highly dubious.

Socialism, communism, capitalism, and mixed economies

In a socialist system, both the means of production and the land are owned by the state, which means that the wealth generated by economic activity is also distributed by the state. Nevertheless, a socialist state may have regular elections and a functional legislative body. The following northern European countries are considered socialist: Romania, Poland, Hungary, Bulgaria, Sweden, Ukraine, Belarus, Russia, and Armenia. The communist system is similar insofar as the means of production and the land are owned by the state, but it is typical for political life to be dominated by one party, often in a totalitarian manner. North Korea, Vietnam, Cuba, and China are all communist countries, though China has successfully introduced some elements of capitalism. The capitalist system places control of the means of production and the land in the hands of private interests. Finally, in a mixed economy, control over the economy is divided between private citizens and the government. In other words, the government controls some functions and leaves others to citizens.

Command and market economies

A command economy is so called because the government decrees that there be specific production levels and prices. This sort of economy is typical of a socialist or communist country (e.g., China, Cuba, North Korea, or Vietnam). In a market economy, on the other hand, the government may interfere slightly, but it mostly leaves economic activity to individual citizens and corporations. In a market economy, the levels of production and prices vary according to supply and demand. Most of the world's industrialized democratic states have market economies. Some of the largest market economies are in western Europe, the United States, and Canada.

China's transition to a market economy

In 1978, the Chinese Communist Party began a program designed to accelerate economic and industrial development. It was called "socialism with Chinese characteristics." Since the initiation of this program, China has gradually shifted toward a market economy. The Chinese government has done this in large part by transferring ownership of industrial concerns from the government to private interests. In fact, private interests are responsible for 70 percent of the country's gross domestic product. At the same time, the Chinese government continues to control many large industries and utilities. This gradual shift from pure communism to an industrial economy has diminished the rate of poverty from 53 percent during the Mao years to a minuscule 6 percent in 2005. Many people have migrated within the country to get jobs in thriving factories, which send products all over the world.

Gorbachev's industrial reform efforts

In its later years, the industrial system of the Soviet Union was full of corruption. Mikhail Gorbachev tried to battle this corruption by giving more authority to factory managers. Instead of having production goals arbitrarily set by the government, the managers would be allowed to make more reasonable predictions. However, the Soviet industrial system had been in decline for so long that workers were not prepared to take on added responsibility. Soviet goods had long been of poor quality, and this trend did not change during Gorbachev's regime. Both managers and workers in Soviet factories were used to having their jobs guaranteed, so they were not accustomed to working hard. In all, Gorbachev's efforts at industrial reform did not create much of an increase in consumption.

Maquiladoras

A "maquiladora" is a factory located in Mexico but near the U.S. border. Because manufacturing costs are much lower in Mexico, many American companies have opted to produce their goods there and then import them back to the United States. Mexican workers are not unionized, so they can be paid less, and the Mexican government does not regulate industry as closely. The proliferation of maquiladoras has drawn many Mexicans north and diminished unemployment in the Mexican nation. Indeed, factory workers in Mexico are fairly well paid compared to the national standard.

State-building

In political science, state-building is the improvement or buttressing of weak or failing states by other states. A successful country does not want to have a weak or failed state on its border because violence and chaos in the adjacent country can easily spill over. Also, the citizens in a weak or failed state will strive to immigrate to neighboring successful states, which can create problems for both economies. There are many ways for a weak or failing state to revive itself, but it usually happens because of a strong leader who is willing to make necessary changes and is able to unify the population, if only for a short time.

Legitimacy and stability

A state is said to have legitimacy when its constitution and government are respected by its citizens and by the leaders of other countries. A legitimate state has citizens who consent to be governed. States that are illegitimate (e.g., Nigeria) have not been able to establish stable governments and therefore do not have the trust of the people and are unable to deal effectively with other countries. States that are continually beset by internal strife and civil war cannot establish legitimacy. A legitimate state has stability, which means that its economy and government cannot be easily overthrown. If a state has a clear and respected system of political operation, it can achieve stability.

- Great Britain: legitimate because even though it does not have a written constitution, it has a competent government and a powerful economy
- Mexico: legitimate because it has an improving economy and a stable government, despite a long history of corruption and one-party rule
- Iran: legitimate, though it may incur sanctions if it continues to pursue a nuclear program; Iran derives legitimacy from the size of its economy and the relative stability of its religious authoritarian government.
- Nigeria: illegitimate because several successive governments have failed there, because the economy is weak, and because there is serious division between the three major ethnic groups
- China: legitimate because its government has been stable for over sixty years and because, despite much government interference, the economy is thriving
- Russia: legitimate because it has a strong government that is battling pervasive corruption

Legitimacy of fascist governments of Germany and Italy

Even the most immoral governments can be legitimate as long as they are stable and respected by their own citizens and the governments of other countries. For instance, during the 1930s and 1940s, the Nazis in Germany and the fascists in Italy achieved legitimacy because they were highly stable and conducted diplomacy with other governments. This legitimacy was achieved despite rampant abuse of human rights by both of these regimes. Similarly, China and Iran are currently considered legitimate even though they are notorious violators of human rights and even though Iran is seeking to obtain nuclear weapons against the protests of the rest of the international community.

Pros and cons of a religious state

In a religious state, there is an officially endorsed religion. In most cases, this is the religious affiliation of the majority of the population. The constitution, the government structure, and the laws of the state are all based on religious principles, from which they derive their legitimacy. It should be noted that in many religious states, citizens are allowed to practice other religions. However, it is common for a religious state to forbid criticism of the government or of the official religion, and religious states are notorious for imposing strict rules on personal conduct. In most cases, as in Iran, religious states are run as autocracies, with the highest political leader being a cleric.

Religious government of Iran

Even though the constitution of Iran names Islam the official state religion, it also permits citizens to practice Judaism, Zoroastrianism, and Christianity. Besides these three, all other religions are forbidden. The most powerful official in the Iranian government is the faqih, who is also the highest religious leader. Nevertheless, Iran does have a legislature and an executive. Even though Iran's government is repressive and outside the mainstream of international relations, it is considered legitimate because it maintains order and stability. Iran's religious government began in 1979 when the shah was overthrown. In the period before the revolution, Iran had been a monarchy.

Ideology and comparison to religious governments

An ideology is a collection of political ideas that organize the structure and behavior of the state or of the particular factions in a state. When a government is based on a particular ideology, as the United States is, it will have a constitution that expresses that ideology. Some common political ideologies are liberalism, conservatism, socialism, communism, and fascism. A religious government, on the other hand, is organized around a set of religious principles rather than a political ideology. Some religious governments have officially enshrined a particular religion as preeminent, while others simply operate as if this had been done. In a religious state, the laws and the structure of government are both based on belief. Both ideological and religious governments can have legitimacy as long as they are respected by their citizens and by other governments.

Liberalism and conservatism

In the classic sense, liberalism is a political philosophy that supports the right of the public to make choices. In recent years, however, it has come to refer to a set of policies that seek to improve the lives of all people by expanding the involvement of the government, often at the expense of personal freedoms. Liberals tend to support entitlement programs, redistribution of wealth, secular government, and equality of outcome for all.

Conservatism, by definition, is an attempt to retain or conserve the way things have been in the past. Conservatives tend to prefer smaller government and place emphasis on personal freedoms rather than using the government as a tool to create an improved society. They also value traditional morals and look to give responsibility to individual citizens and limit the power of government.

Liberals and conservatives of Great Britain
The two main political parties in Great Britain are the Conservative Party and the New Labour Party. Although the New Labour Party was traditionally considered far left, it moved toward the center during Tony Blair's time as prime minister. In its current form, the New Labour Party supports government welfare and healthcare programs, state-sponsored education, regulation of industry, and robust diplomacy. Of course, all these initiatives cost money, so the New Labour Party tends to recommend higher taxes. The Conservative Party, meanwhile, supports lower taxes and a reduction in government spending. The Conservative Party looks to promote free trade, though it opposes joining the European Union and adopting the euro. The Conservative Party is against support for unemployed workers.

Socialist states and communist states

In the socialist and communist systems, the government owns the vast majority of the means of production. Indeed, in communist countries, the government owns all industry. In China, for instance, the government owns the land, though it is willing to lease out some parcels to private farmers. In a communist state, dissent is not tolerated, and the government strictly controls the information available to citizens. Socialist states, on the other hand, do not place all industries under government control. Generally, socialist governments control public services like telephone companies, healthcare providers, and transportation businesses while leaving other industries to be run by private owners. To fund the essential services under government control, the public is typically charged very high taxes in a socialist system.

Communism of the People's Republic of China

In the People's Republic of China, the government is run by a single party, the Communist Party. For much of China's history, communist principles like government ownership of the land and the means of production were sacrosanct. However, some of these restrictions have been eased in recent years, and China has become more capitalist. Nevertheless, even though China allows private ownership and supports foreign investors, it remains avowedly communist. For example, the Chinese government has suppressed all criticism of the communist system, most infamously in the Tiananmen Square massacre of 1989. Suppression of public discourse continues, and in 2000, Google declined to offer some of its services to China amid complaints that the government was using the Internet to crack down on dissidents.

Unitary and federal forms of governance

In a unitary government, power tends to be greatest at the national level. In such a system, there is very little power allocated to the city, county, or state governments. Mainly, these subsidiary governments exist to enforce the laws passed by the main central government. A unitary government is typical of western European countries like France and Germany. In federal systems, there is a more even distribution of power between the national and state governments. In comparative government, these entities are often referred to as the state and substate governments. Some states are allowed to pass laws of their own to deal with problems unique to their territory, but if these laws conflict with federal laws, the federal law usually has precedence. A federal government is typical of countries with a great deal of land and a diverse mixture of ethnic groups.

Parliamentary systems of government and proportional representative systems

The biggest difference between a parliamentary government and a proportional representative government is the manner in which representatives are chosen for the legislature. In a government with proportional representation, voters opt for a political party rather than an individual candidate. Each party receives a number of seats in the legislature proportional to the percentage of votes received. In a proportional representative system, there is more opportunity for small parties. Indeed, it is typical in this system for many small parties to wield significant influence by joining together in a coalition. In a parliamentary system, on the other hand, voters cast their ballots for individual candidates rather than parties. For instance, Great Britain uses a system called single-member district plurality, or "first past the post." In this system, the country is broken up into districts with approximately equal populations. Each party puts forth one candidate for each district. The system is more conducive to a two-party government.

Political accountability

For there to be political accountability, there must be transparency. In government, transparency is the degree to which the public can find out about corruption or misconduct by elected officials. In some constitutional systems, the public has a specific recourse when officials are found to be corrupt: they can order a recall, or emergency election. Of course, in a representative system, the voters can always vote corrupt or ineffective officials out of office eventually. There are also ways for a legislature to monitor itself, typically by holding hearings or investigations or by censuring or dismissing members who have acted unethically. A parliamentary system may give fellow legislators the option of voting "no confidence" with respect to another member.

Political Institutions

EU membership

One of the main advantages of membership in the European Union is freedom from tariffs, or surcharges on the import or export of goods to and from other member countries. Also, commerce is accelerated by the use of a common currency. The EU's legislature is comprised of representatives from each member country. These representatives are elected by the people, though there is little interest in these elections in some countries because the EU is seen as ineffectual. The EU's Charter of Fundamental Rights mandates universal health care and equal pay provisions, and it also bans capital punishment. The EU's Common Agricultural Policy mandates that farmers in all member countries receive the same subsidies, which has annoyed some people by raising the price of goods variously. Finally, the European Court of Justice reviews decisions made in the courts of all member countries.

Regional and local governments

Within a large and diverse country, regions often have a relatively homogenous character, especially with regard to religion and ethnicity. In some cases, the citizens feel more loyalty to the region than to the nation, which can make it difficult for a national government to effectively intervene when there is regional strife. Nigeria is an example of this problem. In other nations, however, citizens maintain regional pride while respecting the authority of the central government. In the United States, for instance, laws passed at the national level have precedence over state laws. The states are usually left to manage things like highways and industrial regulation. Local governments, meanwhile, are responsible for things like police and fire departments and water services.

Unitary and federal governments

The difference between unitary and federal governments has mainly to do with their formation. Federal governments begin when a group of disparate regions join together in a central government. Despite forming this central government, the regions still maintain a decent amount of political power. Some of the countries that have a federal system are Canada, Mexico, Brazil, and the United States. A unitary government, on the other hand, concentrates much more authority in the central government. In a unitary system, political parties are mainly concerned with accumulating national power. In a federal system, political parties are also very concerned with their performance in state and local elections.

Benefits and drawbacks of unitary governments
A unitary government concentrates power in a central authority, such that regional governments are really only responsible for enforcing the laws passed by the central body. A unitary government is most successful when the country is geographically small and has a homogenous population. Unitary governments can be found in Great Britain, France, and other western European nations. One advantage of this government structure is that there is very little conflict between national and regional governments. Most unitary governments are democratic, though it is also possible for them to be communist or socialist.

Centralized and decentralized governments

A centralized government concentrates power in one body. Moreover, a centralized government is typically dominated by a single person, whether an executive or a dictator. This sort of government can go by many different names; for instance, the Communist Party of the Soviet Union described its governing style as "democratic centralism." The system was democratic insofar as members of the government were allowed to discuss issues freely, but government officials were expected to fall in line after a decision had been made. In a decentralized government, power is parceled out to smaller entities, such as the governments of states and municipalities. One advantage of decentralization is that it puts citizens in closer touch with their government and enables government to better respond to local needs. Also, it is more likely that a decentralized government will be able to successfully transfer authority over to private enterprise.

Mexico's decentralized government
In Mexico, a great deal of political power is vested in the state governments. Each state has a governor, a state legislature, and a state police force. Mexicans vote for local offices and elect people to represent their region in the two legislative bodies of the central Mexican government: the Senate and the Chamber of Deputies. Although the structure of the Mexican government is decentralized, the domination of the PRI party concentrated an inordinate amount of power in the central government for much of the country's history. In 2000, with the victory of Vicente Fox, a member of the heretofore marginal PAN party, PRI's rule came to an end.

Centralized government of Iran
The government of Iran is highly centralized, with most of the power vested in the Islamic leader known as the faqih. The central government creates and passes legislation, and the local governments are tasked with enforcing this legislation. The Majlis (legislative body) consists of 290 members who are unaffiliated with any political party, as political parties are illegal in Iran. A set of twelve mullahs, appointed by the faqih and known as the Council of Guardians, delimits the authority of the Majlis. For instance, only candidates approved by the Council of

Guardians may attempt to enter the Majlis, and the Council of Guardians retains the right to veto any legislation it dislikes.

Head of state and head of government

The head of state is the person who represents the state both nationally and internationally. Every type of government has a head of state, though the head of state has no real political power in some cases. For example, the queen is Great Britain's head of state, but her power is entirely ceremonial. The head of government, meanwhile, is the person or small group of people who are really in charge. In some cases, like in the United States, the head of state is the same as the head of government.

Cabinet

The group of advisers chosen by a head of government is called the cabinet. In a parliamentary system, the cabinet of ministers is selected by the prime minister from all the majority party members of parliament. In a parliamentary system, the cabinet makes most of the important decisions. In a federal system, on the other hand, cabinet members are selected by the president and are not necessarily elected officials. The president simply selects those people who he thinks will do the best job. However, members of the president's cabinet must typically undergo a confirmation process in the senate. In America, the members of the president's cabinet are called secretaries (e.g., secretary of state and treasury secretary).

Single versus dual executives

The United States has a single executive: the president. Many other countries, however, have a dual executive system. For instance, France has both a president and a prime minister. In the European Union, executive power is shared by the presidents of the council and the commission. One occasional disadvantage of the dual executive system is that the rival executives will compete for power to the detriment of the country. Also, dual executives may be more likely to develop constituencies within the government to whom they feel beholden. In a single executive system in which the president has the authority to promote legislation and name government officials, the executive's primary responsibility is to the electorate.

President in Iran

In Iran, the president is only the second most powerful politician. The most powerful politician is the supreme leader, or ayatollah, who is the most important Islamic cleric in the nation. The ayatollah is responsible for appointing the top judges, military officials, national security officials, and media members. However, besides making these appointments and influencing decisions behind the scenes, the ayatollah does not participate in day-to-day politics. The Iranian people elect the president, though only candidates approved by the Council of Guardians are allowed to run for this office. Once elected, the president can promote legislation and name new members to the Council of Ministers. The Iranian president is also the primary diplomatic representative of the nation.

Prime minister in Great Britain

In Great Britain, the majority party in the House of Commons elects the prime minister. The prime minister must be a member of the majority party as well as an elected member of the House of Commons. When there is an election in Great Britain, the public generally knows ahead of time who would be selected as prime minister by each party. These days, the prime minister fulfills many of the functions that formerly were the responsibility of the monarch. For example, the prime minister is responsible for promoting and enacting most legislation. Nevertheless, the monarch has so-called "reserve powers," which include the power to act when the security of the country is in question. Indeed, the British monarch has the authority to dismiss the prime minister, though this authority has never been realized.

Functions of a president in Mexico and a prime minister in Great Britain

In Mexico, presidents are limited to a single six-year term. The British prime minister, on the other hand, may stay in office as long as he represents the majority party. However, the prime minister in Great Britain is required to hold elections every five years. Also, a prime minister whose party is defeated may serve as prime minister again in the future should his party regain power. Whereas the prime minister of Britain is selected by the victorious party, the president of Mexico is elected directly by the people. There are some similarities between the British prime minister and the Mexican president, though: both can appoint officials, create and promote legislation, and guide foreign policy. Both of these officials serve as the head of government for their respective nations.

Chief executive officer of the People's Republic of China

In the People's Republic of China, there are three executive positions: general secretary of the Communist Party, chairman of the Chinese Communist Party Central Military Commission, and president of the People's Republic of China. However, above all of these is the paramount leader, who need not hold an explicit position in the Chinese Communist Party. The current paramount leader, Hu Jintao, is also the president of China. Hu was elected to a five-year term by the People's Congress (i.e., not by a popular vote) in 2008. On the other hand, Deng Xiaoping did not hold office in the Chinese Communist Party during his time as paramount leader. Although the paramount leader is the ultimate authority in China, important decisions are also made by the Standing Committee of the Communist Party.

Unicameral and bicameral legislatures

A unicameral legislature has one body, while a bicameral legislature has two. In a bicameral legislature, it is typical for one body to be composed of elected officials from districts of roughly equivalent population or geographic size. This is the case in Britain's House of Commons and the U.S. House of Representatives. The proportional representation in this house is meant to assure representation for all citizens. Usually, the other body in a bicameral system will apportion its members differently. For instance, in the United States and in Mexico, one legislative body contains an equal number of legislators from each state. However, Mexico has begun electing one quarter of its senators according to the party split in a national election. These are not the only ways for legislative bodies to be composed: in Canada, members of the Senate are appointed for life, while in Great Britain, membership in the House of Lords is hereditary.

Iran
The Majlis, Iran's legislative body, is composed of 290 members selected by means of the single-member district plurality system, whereby the country is divided into districts of roughly equal populations. Only candidates who are essentially in line with the views of the Council of Mullahs are allowed to run. Unsurprisingly, those who are elected have very little ability to create meaningful change. Any legislation from the Majlis can be vetoed by the Council of Guardians.

Great Britain
In Great Britain, Parliament is divided into two bodies: an upper House of Lords and a lower House of Commons. The House of Lords is a largely ceremonial body in which membership is hereditary. The House of Lords retains the power to delay legislation from the House of Commons and to initiate bills, though the House of Commons has veto power. The House of Commons is where most legislative action happens. This body can override any veto of the House of Lords. The majority party in the House of Commons selects a prime minister, who then becomes the dominant figure in British politics.

Great Britain's House of Commons consists of 646 Members of Parliament (MPs). The system for electing MPs begins by dividing the country into districts of roughly equivalent populations and geographic areas. These districts are alternately called county and borough constituencies depending on whether they are rural or urban, respectively. Each party runs one candidate per district. MPs serve until the calling of the next election, which cannot be more than five years after the last vote. The House of Lords, meanwhile, has 733 hereditary members. In the future, membership to the House of Lords will be a process of selection rather than inheritance, however.

Russian Federation

Russia has a bicameral legislature: the upper chamber is called the Federation Council of Russia, and the lower chamber is called the Duma. The Duma has 450 members, known as deputies, serving five-year terms. This body is responsible for appointing top-level officials, giving the initial approval for legislation, and ratifying the choice of prime minister. Meanwhile, the Federation Council of Russia is responsible for calling elections, approving the use of military force, and giving the final approval to legislation begun in the Duma. The Federation Council has two members from each of the seventy-four Russian Federation districts.

Nigeria

The bicameral legislature in Nigeria is known as the National Assembly. The lower house, known as the House of Representatives, has 360 members. The top-ranked official in the House of Representatives is the speaker of the House. The upper house of the National Assembly is the Senate, which has 108 members and is led by the president of the Senate. According to the Nigerian constitution, the point of the National Assembly is to "make laws for the peace, order, and good governance of the Federation." The Nigerian legislature was explicitly modeled after that of the United States, and so far it has handled similar legislation.

People's Republic of China

In the People's Republic of China, the legislature is known as the National People's Congress (NPC). Once a year, this body collaborates with the People's National Consultative Conference on important political decisions. These two bodies are collectively known as the "two meetings." In the past, the National People's Congress existed mainly to affirm decisions that had already been made by the Communist Party. However, over the past decade, the NPC has become more openly skeptical of some party decisions. Still, the bills that reach the NPC have already been debated and edited by the Communist Party, and controversial bills rarely reach the NPC at all.

The National People's Congress (NPC) in the People's Republic of China has approximately 3,000 delegates. About 70 percent of these delegates are members of the Communist Party. The process for selecting the delegates to the NPC has several stages. First, each community elects members to a local assembly. Next, local assemblies select delegates for an assembly that covers a larger geographic area. That assembly then selects delegates for an even larger assembly, and so on until a very large assembly selects delegates for the National People's Congress. There are always limitations on the number of candidates for each available seat, and there are usually only a few more candidates than seats. For instance, in provincial elections, there may only be 110 candidates for each hundred available seats. At the local level, the ratio of candidates to seats must be between 120 and 150 percent.

Mexico

Mexico has a bicameral legislature: the upper house is known as the Senate, and the lower house is known as the Chamber of Deputies. Although the Chamber of Deputies is supposed to be responsible for initiating legislation, the vast majority of legislation in Mexico's history has been proposed by the president. The Mexican legislature meets twice a year: from April 15 through July 15 and from November 1 through December 31. When the legislature is not in session, legislative matters are handled by a Permanent Committee. There are 500 representatives in the Chamber of Deputies. Aside from 200 of the members, who are elected by means of a proportional representation system for large districts, the members all serve as the sole representatives of small districts. The members of the Chamber of Deputies serve three-year terms and cannot serve consecutive terms, though they may be reelected after sitting out for a term. The Chamber of Deputies mainly handles domestic affairs like taxes and the budget, but it does have the power to declare war. Most foreign affairs are handled by the Senate, which has 128 members, or four from each of Mexico's thirty-two districts. It is mandatory for one of the four seats in each district to be given to the second-place party.

Separation of powers in parliamentary and presidential systems

In the parliamentary system of government, the prime minister must be a member of the majority party in the legislature. In addition, all the members of the prime minister's cabinet must be elected members of parliament. For this reason, there is greater affinity and cooperation between the executive and legislative branches in a parliamentary system than there is in a presidential system, in which cabinet members need not be drawn from the legislature and the president is elected in a separate contest. In a presidential system, cabinet members are said to serve "at the pleasure of the president," meaning that he can fire cabinet members at any time.

Removal of president or prime minister from office

In a presidential system, such as the one in the United States, legislators can impeach the president, but the president has no authority to oust legislators. Impeachment proceedings are conducted in a manner similar to a trial: both sides of the case are given before the lower house, which then submits the impeachment to a vote. In a parliamentary system, meanwhile, the opposition (minority) party can initiate a vote of "no confidence" at any time. If a majority of the legislators vote no confidence, the prime minister must resign and call an election. This is not the only way for a prime minister to be removed, though. The majority party may also decide at anytime to remove an unsuccessful prime minister.

Party discipline

Party discipline is the uniformity with which the legislators in a political party vote. If all the members of a political party can be persuaded to vote the same way, the party is said to have excellent discipline. In a parliamentary system, it is very important for parties to be disciplined so that they can achieve their legislative goals. If the majority party lacks discipline, it will be easy for the minority party to call for a new election. For this reason, it is rare for a legislator to vote with the opposing party in a parliamentary system.

In a presidential system, there is less emphasis on party discipline. In rare cases, a dissenting legislator may be censured by his own party. However, because there is no opportunity for the minority party to take advantage of fissures in the majority party by calling for a "no confidence" vote, there is less incentive for majority party members to vote as a bloc. In a presidential system, legislators are more conscious of their loyalty to their constituency. When the interests of the constituency conflict with the interests of the party, legislators in a presidential system will often side with the former.

Presidential elections

Nigeria
In the Nigerian national election for president, a candidate must receive a majority (i.e., not a plurality) of the votes and also must receive one-fourth of the votes in at least two-thirds of the states. These rules were put in place to make it more difficult for a single ethnic group to dominate the national government. In legislative races, Nigerians usually have three or more political parties to choose from. There are 360 House districts in Nigeria, each of which is represented by a single member for a four-year term. There are thirty-six Senate districts in Nigeria, each of which is divided into three areas to be represented by a single senator. This means there are 108 senators in all. Nigeria's electoral system is organized fairly well, but it continues to suffer from voter intimidation, fraud, and tampering with ballot boxes.

Mexico
In Mexico, representatives are elected to the Chamber of Deputies for three-year terms according to both plurality and proportional representation methods. Two hundred of the members are elected according to proportional representation, and three hundred are elected according to the plurality, or "first past the post," method. The 160 senators, each of whom serves a four-year term, are also elected by a combination of proportional representation and plurality. In each district, the party that receives the most votes is awarded two seats, and the party that comes in second is guaranteed one seat. Every six years, Mexico elects a president. The president serves a single term and may not run for reelection. Mexico does not have a vice president. The two main political parties

in Mexico are PAN and PRI. The PRI party dominated the country for seventy years, in part, by electoral fraud.

Russian Federation

In Russia, the president is not allowed to serve more than two six-year terms. Before 2008, moreover, each presidential term was only four years. Russia's presidential election has successive levels: when two candidates receive more than 10 percent of the vote in the first election, a runoff is held. The only runoff in the Russian Federation's brief history was in 1996. Russia's legislature, known as the Federal Assembly, is divided into two houses: the Duma and the Federation Council. The Duma is the lower house. It consists of 450 members elected by proportional representation to terms of five years. The upper house, known as the Federation Council, consists of 178 delegates, two from each region of the country. These delegates are appointed, not elected.

Iran

In Iran, the president is elected by a popular vote. To run for this office, candidates must be approved by the Council of Guardians. This is no easy task: in May 2009, the council approved only four of 479 applicants. The 2009 election was further tarnished by allegations of fraud and ballot box stuffing. A recount was performed, but it was also suspect. In the end, the incumbent Mahmoud Ahmadinejad was declared the winner. Candidates for Iran's General Assembly, known as the Majlis, must also obtain approval from the Council of Guardians. Candidates for the legislature run as individuals because they are not allowed to affiliate with political parties.

Elections in Great Britain

In Great Britain, parliamentary elections are held at the request of the ruling party. However, there must be elections at least every five years. Great Britain uses a plurality system, which is conducive to two-party politics. At present, the two most prominent parties in Great Britain are the Conservative Party and the Labour Party. However, the Liberal Democrat Party has gained some momentum in recent years. Parliamentary candidates are typically selected by a party, though anyone can run for office if he obtains ten signatures and pays 500 pounds. In Britain, campaigns tend to be concentrated more on party than individual representatives. The electoral process is initiated when Parliament asks the queen to issue a formal Proclamation of Dissolution of Parliament and Writs of Election. There will be an election seventeen working days after the proclamation is issued. One unique feature of the British electoral system is that departments of the acting government are not allowed to make any abrupt changes or announce any important plans in the six weeks before an election.

Electoral process in the People's Republic of China

In the People's Republic of China, village elections are the bottom rung of the electoral ladder. In these elections, community members select people to represent their interests before the Local Congress of the Chinese Communist Party. Indeed, most of the members of the Local Congress are selected from the delegates in the village assemblies. The top officials in the Local Congress are selected by the Communist Party, which is by far the most important party in China. The leader of China is known as the paramount leader; in most cases, this individual is also the nominal leader of the Communist Party.

Referenda

A referendum queries the voting public on a particular issue. Either the legislature or a group of citizens may initiate a referendum. In many cases, a certain number of citizens must sign a petition for a referendum to take place. Typical subjects for referenda are impeachment proceedings, international treaties, or constitutional amendments. In some political cultures, referenda are used often, even on such matters as taxation and federal expenditures. A binding referendum takes the will of the people as a command. A nonbinding referendum, on the other hand, is simply used to gauge public opinion; it may be honored or dismissed. In some cases, a binding referendum needs a supermajority (i.e., some amount greater than half the vote). In addition, some countries require a certain number of voters for a referendum to take effect.

Noncompetitive elections

Authoritarian or totalitarian governments may hold sham elections to create an appearance of propriety or to "ratify" the dictator or head of state. Sometimes, the military or police force intimidates voters at the polls. Although such an election underscores the unfairness of politics under a brutal regime, it at least demonstrates the ruling faction's desire to appear legitimate internationally. Some noncompetitive elections give a small part of the electorate a choice. In China, for instance, village members have some influence over their delegates to the village council. After that point, however, the delegates for successive and larger assemblies are selected by party members rather than by the electorate.

Proportional representation election process

In a proportional representation system, voters select a political party rather than an individual candidate. Each party gets a number of seats in the legislature proportionate to its percentage of the total vote. In a proportional representation system, there is no risk of narrow victories in many districts, giving disproportionate power to a party that lost the popular vote. The proportional representation system allocates representatives to every political party that gets a share of the vote, which encourages a large number of parties. To exert influence, smaller parties must form a coalition.

Single-member district representation

In a single-member district representation system, each political party nominates one candidate per district, and each district contains approximately the same number of people. Whichever candidate achieves the majority wins. Sometimes this system is called "first past the post" because the difference of even a single vote is enough to make a candidate victorious. One of the disadvantages of the single-member district representation system is that minority parties may have a hard time gaining a footing. This system is conducive to two-party politics. Because only the candidate with the most votes wins, voters may be reluctant to vote for a candidate who seems highly unlikely to win. Single-member district representation voting guarantees that the majority will run the government.

Alternative versions
One of the variations of single-member district voting is called the single transferable vote system. In it, all the candidates from each party are grouped together on the ballot, and voters opt for one group of candidates. Another variation of single-member district voting is the closed-list system, which gives voters a choice of policy proposals rather than named candidates. In the open-list system, candidates and party affiliations are on the ballot, and voters may either vote entirely for one party or for a mix of individual candidates.

Organization of political parties

The manner in which political parties are organized varies according to the election system. Great Britain and the United States use a first-past-the-post system, which encourages two-party politics. China has essentially a single-party system in which only the Communist Party may operate. Countries that have preferential or proportional representation systems typically have room for three or more viable political parties. Regardless of the election system, a party is generally organized around a particular ideology. As an example, the New Labour Party is focused on economic growth and the bolstering of the middle class in Great Britain. The ideology of a party may change to win votes; after all, a political party cannot achieve any part of its agenda if it does not run successful campaigns.

Political party membership

A political party seeks to attract voters who share the party's ideology. Sometimes, however, people join a political party because of their interest in a specific issue. Political parties take active steps, through television and print advertising, to attract new members. The Internet is also a crucial meeting place and organizational hub for political parties. Local parties need the financial support of members to run campaigns and distribute campaign literature. The more money a political party has, the greater influence it will have in the government. Political parties also encourage their members to contact legislators and lobby for specific bills.

Party institutionalization

Party institutionalization occurs when the general public accepts and agrees with the ideology and intentions of a political party. When this occurs, those core values or policies may be enshrined in law. In political science, there are four components of political institutionalization: roots in society, level of organization, autonomy, and coherence. To have roots in society means that a political party must recognize and honor the basic traditions of the citizens. The level of organization is the degree of hierarchy and the uniformity of purpose within a political party. Autonomy is a party's freedom from influence by lobbyists or special interests; a political party that can demonstrate autonomy is more likely to gain the trust of its members. Finally, a party's platform must be coherent for it to be adopted by the general public. This means that a party's literature and its representatives must do a good job of clearly stating the party's policies.

Political ideology and liberalism and conservatism

Political ideology is the principles or ideals that guide the rhetoric and actions of a political party. An ideology usually includes goals as well as a plan for achieving those goals. Liberalism is an ideology focused on ameliorating life for common citizens. Liberals are more likely to propose and support radical solutions to contemporary problems. For instance, British Liberal Democrats advocate the adoption of the euro because they believe this would simplify trade and stimulate the economy. Though all liberals are described as being on the "left," the concerns of liberals in different countries may be quite diverse.Conservatism is an ideology concerned with maintaining the traditional state of political life. For example, British Conservatives oppose the adoption of the euro because they prefer the economic strength and stability of the pound.

Ideologies of major political parties

Great Britain
In recent history, Great Britain has been dominated by the New Labour Party and the Conservative Party. The New Labour Party arose out of the socialist groups and powerful trade unions of the nineteenth century. It was first founded to represent the interests of the working class, though now its concerns are more in line with those of the middle class. Moreover, the New Labour Party has eschewed socialism in favor of a free-market economic plan. The Conservative Party, meanwhile, is to the right of New Labour. It tends to oppose major economic innovations, such as joining the European Union. The Conservative Party has fought to keep Scotland in Great Britain and has supported environmental initiatives, education, the Home Office, and the National Health Service. In recent years, the Liberal Democrat Party has become a more viable third party. With a motto of "change that works for you," the Liberal Democrats have pursued fair taxes, green jobs, quality education, and a reduction in government corruption.

Iran
Only avowedly Islamic political parties are allowed in Iran. There are five at present:
- Executives of Construction Party: a group of reformers that is highly critical of current Iranian President Mahmoud Ahmadinejad
- Islamic Iran Participation Front: committed to the advancement of democracy in Iran. For this reason, its candidates have frequently been forbidden from running for office by the Council of Guardians. The slogan of the party is "Iran for Iranians."
- Islamic Society of Engineers: explicitly committed to "elevating the Islamic, political, scientific, and technical knowledge of the Muslim people of Iran, defending major freedoms such as freedom of expression and gatherings, as well as continued campaigning against foreign cultural agents, whether Eastern or Western materialism"
- Militant Clergy Association: a moderate party made up of conservative clerics
- Militant Clerics Society: Committed to "exporting the revolution," this extremist group promotes total state control of the economy.

China
Although the Chinese Constitution does not forbid the existence of other political parties, the Communist Party has dominated the country's leadership for its entire history. The avowed goal of the Chinese Communist Party is development of the economy through "socialism with Chinese characteristics." The party also has a strong interest in preserving Chinese culture and promoting communism. One characteristic feature of the Chinese Communist Party has been the "mass line," whereby government aid is delivered to villages and small agricultural

communities. The party has done a good job of encouraging interest in local politics through village elections and councils.

Nigeria
In Nigeria, the most powerful political party is the People's Democratic Party, which promotes the free market and opposes government intervention in the economy. However, this party recently backed a national health insurance initiative. Regarding social issues, the People's Democratic Party supports religious freedom but is intolerant of homosexuality. One major issue in Nigeria is the distribution of oil revenue: the People's Democratic Party supports continuation of the present balance of payments. There are fifty-four other parties in Nigeria, many of which represent ethnic or religious groups rather than political ideologies. In February 2010, twenty-five of these parties discussed forming a larger group with the rather vague platform of "good government, economic prosperity, and social justice."

Mexico
In Mexico, the long-dominant PRI party has had a notoriously vague policy platform. The party often shifted its ideology according to the whims of the voters. Since losing the presidency in 2000, the PRI platform has become even more nebulous. PRI currently defines itself as a centrist party. PAN, meanwhile, has a more consistent reputation for moderate conservatism. However, implicit in the party's name (National Action) is the idea that pragmatic solutions are more important than ideological theories to this party. In general, the PAN party seems to favor the free market and a reduction of government interference in the economy. Also, PAN is a Christian party that opposes homosexuality and abortion. PRD, finally, is a more leftist party that tends to support economic nationalism, social justice, and welfare programs.

European Union
The ideology of the European Union (EU) is laid out in the Charter of Fundamental Rights, which guarantees certain rights like health care and equal pay for equal work. The Treaty of Lisbon of 2009, which is in essence the EU constitution, refined the body's ideology by promoting women's rights, forbidding torture, and expressing a desire to promote common values. All EU member countries are obliged to abide by the terms of the Charter of Fundamental Rights.

Multiparty system

A multiparty political system is more typical of a country with a high degree of cultural, ethnic, and religious diversity. When there are many political parties, the government's decisions tend to reflect that diversity. Political parties are also forced to cooperate much more in a multiparty system because no one party has enough power to dominate. Although minorities are well represented in a multiparty system, it can be difficult to assemble a working coalition. This type of system is notoriously unstable.

Party systems

Great Britain
Great Britain's "first-past-the-post" electoral system is conducive to two-party politics, and for the past few decades, the British Parliament has been dominated by the Conservative and New Labour parties. There are no other large parties, though the leftist Liberal Democrats have gained some strength lately. After forming a government, the ruling party must call another election within five years. When the ruling party feels confident of reelection, it is typical for an election to be called after four years. In an odd paradox of the British system, unpopular governments that have been formed for four years are apt to wait an extra fifth year in the hopes that public approval will rise.

China
Even though China's constitution establishes a multiparty political system, in practice the government has been dominated by the Communist Party since its inception. In 2007, China's State Council Information Office declared that the Communist Party is at the head of a "multiparty cooperation and political consultation system." Although China does have eight other political parties, the aim of these parties is not to win power so much as to assist the Communists with the development of Chinese socialism. The Chinese government justifies this unorthodox political system by pointing to China's unique traditions and culture. Most critics, however, argue that China only maintains the appearance of a multiparty system to avoid censure by the international community. Nevertheless, the Chinese government has remained remarkably stable throughout its history.

Iran
The most powerful figure in Iranian politics is the ayatollah, though the country also has an elected president and legislature. The 1979 Iranian constitution permitted political parties, "provided they do not violate the principles of independence, freedom, national unity, criteria of Islam, or the basis of the Islamic Republic." To run for a seat in the legislature, citizens must receive the approval of the Council of Guardians. This council is extremely strict and does not allow any potential reformers to run for office. At present, the following political parties are active in Iran: the Moderation Front and Executives of Construction Party, a weak party in support of centrist politics; the Participation Front, a party that tries to raise political participation among citizens; the Militant Clerics Association, a group of relatively leftist religious leaders; and the National Trust Party, an organization that vows to defend the rights of the people and to scrutinize government actions. None of these parties wield much power in Iran, and any legislation they are able to pass can be vetoed.

Mexico

In 1917, Mexico drafted a constitution that allowed the formation of political parties, yet the country was dominated for more than seventy years by a single party: the Institutional Revolutionary Party (PRI). The success of this party was due both to savvy political maneuvering and to more nefarious means, including corruption, election fraud, and bribery. For many years, PRI was unsuccessfully opposed by the National Action Party (PAN), but a PAN candidate for state governor was elected in 1989, and PAN candidate Vicente Fox was elected president in 2000. Since then, the balance between PRI and PAN has been further complicated by the rise of the Democratic Revolutionary Party (PRD) and the Ecologist Green Party (PVEM).

Nigeria

In Nigeria, there are about fifty political parties. However, only eight of these parties had representatives in the National Assembly after the most recent elections in 2007. The People's Democratic Party has 54.5 percent of the seats in the House and 53.7 percent of the seats in the Senate. The second most prominent party is the All Nigeria People's Party. Besides these two, the remaining six represented parties each received less than 1 percent of the vote. Some Nigerian legislators believe there are too many parties, and they have proposed a bill to limit the number of parties to two or three. Such a bill might make it easier to form a consensus. Ironically, the Nigerian constitution of 1999 encouraged a two-party system by requiring presidential candidates to earn more than 50 percent of the popular vote and to receive at least 25 percent of the vote in two-thirds of the states.

Russia

On April 13, 2010, the Russian Federation enacted a new constitution that had been approved by popular referendum. This constitution increased executive power and encouraged multiparty politics. It requires parties to earn 7 percent of the popular vote to be represented in the Duma or the Federal Council. During Putin's regime, there was a movement to reform elections and eliminate some of the country's forty-six political parties. In the 2007 elections, seven parties combined for 63.9 percent of the vote. Interestingly, parties are only minor players in electoral politics in Russia. Many people do not know the major party platforms, and presidential candidates like Yeltsin and Putin won as independents.

European Union

The European Union is a supranational organization, meaning that it is a collaboration among sovereign nations. In this case, member nations collaborate with the goal of mutual economic benefit. Though the European Union has a parliament, the members represent nations rather than political parties. Each nation holds elections for these seats. For a long time, seats in the EU Parliament were allocated according to population, but the present system gives more seats to the older member nations. In a sense, nations play the roles of parties: they advocate for their particular constituencies. Delegates to the EU often oppose measures that would diminish the sovereignty of their respective home nations.

Elite recruitment

Elite recruitment is the system for filling positions of power and influence in the government. A version of this process occurs in every political system. In Great Britain, elite recruitment depends on the electoral process because only members of the ruling party in Parliament can fill cabinet positions. In the United States, on the other hand, the president can fill his cabinet with men and women from the private sector. The process of composing a nation's elite is extremely important because these people will be responsible for making the most significant decisions. Also, many of the people who are recruited into the elite will remain there long after the end of the regime that recruited them.

National leadership and processes of elite recruitment

Iran
There is a considerable difference between the way Iran claims to compose its elite and the way it actually does. Whatever appearances there may be to the contrary, the most important political actor in the country is the supreme religious leader. He has the power to command security police, overrule court decisions, declare war, and control the media. The selection of the supreme leader is made by a collection of eighty-six religious leaders, each of whom is elected to an eight-year term. This group is responsible for the vast majority of Iran's elite recruitment because it selects the supreme religious leader and decides who may run for office.

People's Republic of China
The head of the Chinese government, known as the paramount leader, is often but not always the general secretary of the Communist Party. However, anyone who becomes paramount leader automatically takes control of the party. In addition, the paramount leader is in charge of the Central People's Government and the People's Liberation Army. Over the past decade, the Standing Committee of the Communist Party has taken on more power. The process of selecting a new paramount leader begins when the current leader hands over the office of general secretary of the Communist Party. After this, the chosen successor becomes president of the country and then chairman of the Central Military Commission. The only path to elite status in China is through early and diligent membership in the Communist Party.

Mexico

For as long as the PRI party was dominant, the process of selecting a new Mexican leader went according to the tradition of "dedazo," or finger-pointing. In other words, the next PRI candidate would be selected by the current president without the formality of a primary or nominating convention. Other parties, most notably PAN, would run candidates in the general election, but they always lost. In many cases, the general elections were rife with voter fraud and corruption. In 2000, the PAN presidential candidate Vicente Fox was elected. Since then, elections in Mexico have mainly been free and fair.

Nigeria

Although Nigeria ostensibly has a parliamentary system in which a president and vice president are elected, the country has continually struggled with corruption and electoral fraud. Most recently, in January 2010, Nigeria experienced a constitutional crisis when the elected president, Alhaji Umaru Yar'Adua, became ill and there was no protocol for passing authority to the vice president, Goodluck Jonathan. The process of elite recruitment in Nigeria has often been marked by ethnic favoritism. Although Nigeria aspires to be a meritocracy, education and other qualifications have rarely been the most important factors in hiring and appointments. In recent years, federal government jobs have become even more valuable, as the central government has farmed out many of its duties to regional offices. Because Nigeria's economy continues to struggle, relatively lucrative positions in the government are highly sought after.

Great Britain

Great Britain's most important political figure is the prime minister, who must be a member of the ruling party in Parliament. Although the king or queen is the nominal leader of the British government, he has a merely ceremonial role at this point. Britain's elite recruitment process is somewhat restricted, as the prime minister may only choose elected members of the ruling party for his cabinet. Moreover, the prime minister serves at the pleasure of his party and can be voted out by his party at anytime.

Russian Federation

In the Russian Federation, there is a president and a prime minister, though there is no vice president. The president, who is elected by the general public, selects the prime minister and the members of the presidential cabinet. Russia has a bicameral legislature composed of the Duma and the Federation Council. The president may dissolve the Duma and submit laws to popular referendum whenever he chooses. The Russian president is also responsible for appointing top government officials and department ministers. The current president, Dmitry Medvedev, has filled his administration with successful businessmen.

Interest groups

An interest group is organized around the purpose of advancing a particular cause. Although many interest groups, like labor unions, are largely apolitical, they may occasionally participate in political discourse. Some interest groups represent narrow constituencies, like auto workers, while others represent large causes or groups, like civil rights or senior citizens. One of the main activities of interest groups is lobbying, in which they attempt to persuade legislators to adopt their agenda. In democracies, interest groups are not only allowed, but are considered a valuable part of political discourse. In authoritarian countries, however, the role of interest groups is necessarily limited.

Interest group systems
An interest group system is a collection of interest groups that join together to increase their influence over government. In the United States, for example, all the major automotive manufacturers combine their lobbying efforts. This process is similar to the dynamic in a proportional representation system: there are many different groups that have overlapping desires, so they improve their odds of getting what they want by combining their power. It is very common for an interest group to cooperate with similar groups in some areas and then to act alone in other areas.

Economic interest groups, cause groups, and public interest groups
An economic interest group focuses on business and financial issues. Some common economic interest groups are labor unions, farm representatives, business groups, and industrial concerns. A cause group is focused on a particular moral issue, usually social in nature. For instance, in the United States, there are strong cause groups on either side of the abortion issue. A public interest group has a broader focus, such as government oversight or environmental protection. Because its interests are more expansive, a public interest group is likely to extend its lobbying efforts beyond national borders.

Private and public institutional interest groups and nonassociated interest groups
Technically, private and public institutional interests are not interest groups because they consist of organizations or government departments rather than private citizens. In authoritarian countries, there is usually no point in economic and cause groups, so institutional interest groups are likely to be prevalent and relatively influential. A nonassociated interest group is a more informal collection of people who rally together for a particular transient cause. For example, the "green movement" in Iran arose in response to perceived election fraud in 2009.

Advantages

By joining an interest group, an individual increases his ability to influence government. Interest groups provide a number of services that a single citizen cannot. For example, interest groups maintain a steady correspondence with elected officials, making sure that legislators and executives have all the relevant information on particular issues. Also, interest groups help recruit and support candidates who are in line with their goals, a function that is obviously beyond the power of most private citizens. Interest groups can organize propaganda and get-out-the-vote campaigns very effectively. In some cases, as in authoritarian regimes, powerful leaders use interest groups to create the appearance of support for government policies.

Factors affecting interest group creation

Wealthy countries that have thriving economies are more likely to have a great number of interest groups. In part, this is because wealthy countries have more citizens who can donate to interest groups, and wealthy governments have more to offer interest groups. Poor countries tend to have few and ineffective interest groups. In authoritarian countries, interest groups may not be allowed at all. The operations of interest groups are in large part dependent on the structure of government. In a parliamentary system like that of Great Britain, there are hundreds of legislators who could be targeted by lobbyists. In an authoritarian regime, there are really only a few people who have influence over government decisions. In the United States, state and local governments have considerable power, which means that they are frequently lobbied by interest groups.

Theory of pluralism

The political theory of pluralism is the idea that politics operates like a marketplace in which all groups have an equal opportunity to make their case. In other words, nobody is excluded from political debate and from attempting to influence those in power. The United States, Australia, and Canada have all tried to create pluralist political environments. However, there are inevitable disparities in influence when some interest groups are better funded than others. In addition, elected officials will be naturally more sympathetic to some issues than to others, so some interest groups will be inherently favored.

Neo-corporatism and state corporatism theories

Neo-corporatist theory asserts that the state should function like a carefully structured corporation. The government, labor interests, and members of the business community should all cooperate to ensure that the goals of the nation are met. States that operate on the neo-corporatist model will try to maintain low expenditures and low inflation rates in the hopes of supporting a high standard of living for their citizens and carrying on effective trade relations with other nations. Some of the most successful neo-corporatist states are Scandinavian countries like Sweden and Norway. These countries have high taxes, but they maintain a high quality of living for their citizens. In a neo-corporatist state, interest groups must be very strategic. For instance, Japan's neo-corporatist state claims to represent the interests of workers and therefore excludes labor unions. In state corporatism, meanwhile, all the elements of business, labor, and regulation are managed by the government. State corporatism is almost synonymous with authoritarian rule.

Lobbying

One of the primary activities of interest groups is lobbying, or the attempted persuasion of government officials. Lobbying is an art rather than a science, and its practice depends in large part on the structure of government. Lobbyists try to develop positive relationships with government officials, often by making contributions to political campaigns. Of course, lobbying is much more successful in a democracy than in an authoritarian state. In a one-party or authoritarian state, lobbyists are more apt to take on subservient relationships to all-powerful government officials.

Varying approaches
The most successful lobbyists usually come from long-established and large interest groups. Successful lobbyists have extensive connections in government. When a new interest group is formed, it often takes years for it to establish useful connections in government. Some organizations have to adjust their policies and ideals to make their lobbying efforts more fruitful. In particular, new interest groups may focus on small-scale versions of reform before they begin lobbying for major changes. New interest groups are likely to spend a considerable amount of time on telephone and direct mail campaigns.

Main strategies in different political systems
In an authoritarian society, lobbying is generally frowned upon and must take place behind the scenes. For this reason, lobbying is likely to include bribery. In a democracy, however, lobbying can take place in view of the public. In addition, lobbyists in a democracy are free to make use of a wider range of marketing tools, including demonstrations and direct mail campaigns. In a parliamentary democracy, lobbyists focus their attention on the prime minister and his cabinet. In the United States, on the other hand, a great deal of lobbyists' energy is directed at legislators and officials in the state and local governments. Outside of the United States, professional lobbyists are largely scorned. In Europe, it is much more common for the government to do business directly with interest groups than to use lobbyists as liaisons.

Defeating proposed legislations and laws
A significant amount of lobbying aims at defeating proposed legislation and rescinding existing laws. In the United States, lobbyists target those legislators who they believe will be receptive to their message. If a law has already been passed by the legislature, a lobbyist may try to convince the executive to use his veto power. In a parliamentary system, it is much more difficult to get the ruling party to eliminate proposed legislation that was a core part of the party's

campaign platform. For this reason, lobbyists may spend more of their time trying to have legislation adjusted than defeated. In an authoritarian system, finally, it may be almost impossible for lobbyists to stop the passage of proposed legislation. The only hope for lobbyists in this kind of political system is their strong relationship with powerful government officials.

Bureaucracy

A bureaucracy is an organizational structure within a large institution. The overarching goal of a bureaucracy is efficiency. To this end, bureaucracies promote specialization, hierarchy, and rigid adherence to rules. There are generally multiple ascending layers of employees: workers are supervised by managers, who in turn are supervised by department managers, and so on up to the executive. Although the word *bureaucracy* has become synonymous with overcomplexity and inflexibility, there are plenty of examples of efficient and successful bureaucracies. For instance, the British civil service is a meritocracy with a generally positive history. Indeed, the stability of the British civil service system has maintained continuity in the provision of services even after elections, when the incoming party tends to appoint relatively inexperienced bureau chiefs.

Max Weber outlines seven principles in the operation of all bureaucracies:
  1. and 2. The official business of bureaucracies is accomplished according to three rules:
  - Every employee has a specialized job.
  - Every employee has the authority to do that job.
  - Every employee has an explicit and limited means of coercion.
  3. Every employee is part of the bureaucratic hierarchy. He is supervised, as are his supervisors, and there is a clear channel for appeal.
  4. Employees do not own—but are responsible for—the resources they use in their work.
  5. Private income is distinct from official income.
  6. No jobs can be sold or inherited.
  7. Official business is based on documentation.

Coercive organization

A coercive organization is one that forces people to join it. An extreme example of a coercive organization is prison, as very few people volunteer to serve time there. Another way of defining a coercive organization is as a body that forces its members to do things they might prefer not to. In this respect, the military is an example of a coercive organization. Members of the military have a specific mission: to follow the order of their commanders and to protect their nation. This might sometimes require them to do unpleasant things. The military can become an even more coercive organization when it tries to take over the civil government. In that case, the nation's military is forcing citizens to abide by its rules involuntarily.

Iran

There are several coercive organizations in Iran. The most prominent of these is the Council of Guardians, which determines who is allowed to run for legislative seats. The Council of Guardians is a group of twelve men selected by the Supreme Court and the supreme leader. Besides being able to select who can run for office, the Council of Guardians can also veto any legislation it dislikes. Another coercive element of the Iranian government is the supreme leader, who has sole power to select judges, command the military, and manipulate the media. Some critics of Iran would even designate Islam itself as a coercive organization there because it establishes a set of nonnegotiable rules that all Iranian citizens must follow.

Nigeria

Since 1966, when the military ousted what it claimed was a corrupt government, Nigeria has endured several bouts of martial law. Until 1979, most Nigerians appreciated the stability of military rule despite the violence that followed the attempted secession of the Igbos in 1967. General Obasanjo restored civilian government in 1979 and created what came to be known as the Second Republic. This government proved no more able to avoid rampant bribery (known in Nigeria as "dash") and tribal favoritism (known as "chop politics") than the government it replaced. In 1985, the military again took control. The military ruled until 1998 when General Abacha died. The government then reverted to chaotic civilian rule in the so-called Fourth Republic.

People's Republic of China

One of the most coercive policies in an exceptionally coercive political system has been the Chinese Communist Party's regulation of family size. China's baby boom during the 1940s was cheered at first; by 1955, however, the government realized there were too many citizens to feed. That year, the Chinese government came out in favor of birth control, which it had previously prevented from entering the country in 1949. In 1979, the Chinese Communist Party went so far as to declare that families could only have one child. Those who broke the rules and had a second child were forced to pay a stiff fine and potentially undergo forced sterilization. In exchange for having only a single child, first-time mothers received maternity benefits and a certificate of honor. *Time* magazine estimates that this policy has prevented at least 250 million births. This policy has also had other unpleasant side effects, namely the abortion of female babies. Female babies are seen as less valuable than their male counterparts in China. There are now far more males than females in China. For this reason, in 1994, the Chinese government forbade parents from learning the gender of their baby before birth.

All the land and means of production in China are owned by the government, which means that people can be evicted at anytime. As the government has converted farmland into factories, many Chinese people have been kicked out of their farms and homes. Those who have been evicted have no recourse under Chinese law. Another classic example of coercion by the Chinese government is the Tiananmen Square massacre of 1989 in which protesting students were violently suppressed.

Judicial systems

People's Republic of China
The autonomy of a country's judiciary is usually explicit in the country's constitution. In China, the judiciary is said to have complete autonomy. In practice, though, the courts are heavily dominated by the Communist Party. The Chinese constitution divides the court system into four levels. There are special courts for forestry, water systems, infrastructure, and the military. There is a set of intermediate courts that handles parochial issues in small towns and counties. Above these is a set of lower courts that handles cases in small cities and districts. The largest court in China is the Supreme People's Court in Beijing.

Russian Federation
The Constitution of the Russian Federation declares that there will be an independent judiciary, including a Supreme Court, Constitutional Court, and Supreme Court of Arbitration. In 2009, though, in an interview with a Spanish newspaper, Judge Vladimir Yaroslavtsev complained that the executive branch and the Russian security service had infringed on the rights of the judiciary. Soon after, Yaroslavtsev was accused by the Constitutional Court of undermining judicial authority. He was forced to resign, as was another judge, Anatoly Kononov, who supported his claim.

Nigeria
Nigeria's 1999 constitution established a judiciary with federal and state courts, courts of appeal, and a federal Supreme Court. In addition, there are traditional courts of appeal and an Islamic court of appeal. A case is only heard in the traditional or Islamic court of appeal if both the plaintiff and the defendant agree. Nevertheless, these courts are often chosen because they are more convenient for rural citizens and tend to be less expensive. Unfortunately, these regional traditional and Islamic courts are beset by corruption and bribery. In 1998 and 1999, during the rule of Abdulsalami Abubakar, there were several military tribunals, which functioned as courts despite the lack of official sanction. Although many Nigerians complain of corruption and political influence in the court system, there is no hard evidence of a lack of autonomy in the judiciary.

Mexico

Mexico has a judiciary with special courts, circuit courts, circuit tribunals, and a Supreme Court. There are no jury trials in Mexico, so judges are responsible for rendering decisions and levying sentences. According to the Writ of Amparo, those who are convicted in a local court can appeal to a federal court. Other than federal judges, who receive lifetime appointments, members of the Mexican judiciary serve six-year terms. Despite the establishment of an independent judiciary by the Mexican Constitution of 1917, there are still frequent accusations of political influence in the courts. The Mexican tradition of "mordida," or bribery, has survived partly because judges receive fairly low salaries. Most observers believe that the judiciary has become more independent since the end of PRI domination in 2000.

Iran

The Iranian legal code is based on sharia, or Islamic law. The supreme leader of Iran appoints the head of the judiciary and has the ability to replace him at anytime. According to the Iranian constitution, the top-ranking members of the judiciary are the Supreme Court and the High Council of the Judiciary, which has four members. The Iranian judiciary is composed of seventy revolutionary courts and many other public courts, courts of peace, and Supreme Courts of Cassation. To be a judge, one must be certified in Islamic law. In Iran, the judge acts both as prosecutor and jury. The constitution of Iran claims to establish an independent judiciary, but like all parts of the Iranian government, it is subject to the influence of the supreme leader, who has the authority to replace judges and overturn judicial decisions on a whim.

Great Britain

Great Britain's parliamentary system is divided into three branches: legislative, executive, and judicial. These distinctions are not enshrined in a written constitution, but they are instead backed by 800 years of precedent and case law. The highest court of appeal in Great Britain is the upper house of Parliament, the House of Lords. This unusual system has been criticized by the European Union. Although judicial appointments are technically made by the monarch, they are in fact made by the Prime Minister. Most British judges have worked previously as solicitors (lawyers who represent private citizens) and barristers (lawyers authorized to argue before superior courts). In the British system, the top judicial officials are the attorney general, solicitor general, and lord chancellor. Despite the popular opinion that the British judicial system should maintain absolute autonomy, Parliament retains the right to overturn decisions made by the judiciary.

European Union

The European Union's judicial system is called the European Court of Justice. It is composed of one judge from each EU member state. The point of this court is to interpret the laws and supervise their enforcement in member countries. To this end, the court scrutinizes decisions made in the courts of member countries. Although its actual authority is limited to EU operations, the European Court of Justice has absolute autonomy.

Judicial review

Great Britain, Iran, and Mexico

Judicial review is a unique process in Great Britain because the country does not have a formal constitution with which decisions can be compared. The judicial review process is only applied to legislative and executive decisions. According to the doctrine of parliamentary sovereignty, the legislature has the final say about the legality of policies and laws. In Mexico, the Supreme Court was given the power of judicial review as part of a series of constitutional changes enacted by President Ernest Zedillo in 1994. Although the purpose of this reform was probably to increase the power of the PRI party, the strategy ended up backfiring in 1988 when a judicial review action ruled against PRI. Finally, Iran's judicial review system entails a panel of certified Islamic judges that determines whether a policy or piece of legislation is aligned with sharia law.

Russia, Nigeria, and China

In Russia, there is a complex system of regional constitutional courts; these regional courts are charged with aligning local laws and court judgments with the national constitution. Russia's Supreme Court does not have the right of judicial review, though there is a national constitutional court that has this power. In Nigeria, the 1999 constitution gave the power of judicial review to the Supreme Court, though many observers are highly dubious of the court's ability to exercise this power impartially. The intention of the judicial review process in Nigeria is to safeguard human rights and to determine the constitutionality of government actions. The People's Republic of China establishes judicial review, though this power is somewhat diminished by the Communist Party's ability to override court decisions. Furthermore, only the most important legal issues are considered worthy of judicial review.

European Union

In the European Union, the Court of Justice has the power of judicial review over the decisions made in the courts of member countries as well as over the laws passed by the legislatures of member countries. The intention of the judicial review process in the EU is to ensure that legislation in member countries is aligned with the laws of the EU. The Court of Justice only has the power of judicial review over the national courts of member countries. Also, the citizens of member countries may not appeal judgments in their own courts to the Court of Justice. When a national court wants a ruling related to EU law, it can appeal to the Court of Justice. After the EU Court of Justice has made a ruling, national courts are charged with enforcing the decision. Although there is no direct way to mandate obedience, member countries are bound by honor to accept the rulings of the Court of Justice.

Types of law

Great Britain
There are three types of law in Great Britain: common law, statute law, and European law. Common law has been established and refined by centuries of case study and precedent. The common laws of Great Britain are traditional, and they are often not written down. In large part, common law depends on the history of court rulings on a particular subject. Statute law is created, along with statutory instruments, by Parliament. Statutory instruments are like bureaucratic rules or regulations, and they are typically offered by the ministers in charge of particular civil service departments. Finally, as a member of the EU, Britain has pledged to honor European law. In some cases, European law takes precedence over the statutes of Parliament.

People's Republic of China
The constitution of China outlines the validity of all the major types of law used in other countries (e.g., criminal law, tax law, and antitrust law). China also has an extensive set of statutes related to martial law, or the temporary use of military force domestically to quell uprisings. For instance, in 1989, China declared martial law during the protests in Tiananmen Square. Approximately 1,400 demonstrators were killed, and many more were jailed. Typically, martial law ends as soon as the immediate crisis has been handled.

Nigeria
There are two unusual types of law in Nigeria: sharia law and customary law. Sharia law is another name for Islamic law, though it extends beyond religious issues to general conduct. Sharia law is especially present in the Muslim-dominated areas of northern Nigeria. Customary law descends from tribal law and is concerned mainly with inheritance, marriage, and the acquisition of land. To maintain their validity in modern Nigeria, customary laws must pass a repugnancy test, meaning they must demonstrate that they are not repugnant to justice, natural law, or good conscience. The other laws in Nigeria are mainly based on British law. For instance, Nigeria has a set of common laws, a set of court statutes, and a body of legislation passed since 1999. Nigeria retains some of the military law that was developed during various periods of past military rule. These holdovers from previous regimes are called existing laws.

Iran

Iranian law is mostly sharia. The legislature established by Iran's constitution may only pass laws that conform with sharia law, which is based on the Koran. Religious authorities claim that sharia law is infallible and cannot be modified. However, many people feel that punishments like caning and dismemberment for criminal offenses are violations of human rights. Iran is often in conflict with the international Court of Justice because of controversy over Iranian court rulings.

Mexico

Because Mexico's constitution of 1917 did not acknowledge the diverse ethnic groups that make up the Mexican population, President Carlos Salinas amended the constitution in 1992 to permit indigenous people to honor their own legal practices and customs, most of which deal with land management. The rest of the Mexican legal system is outlined in the 1917 constitution. One idiosyncratic element of Mexican law is so-called "social law." There are five basic codes in Mexican law: civil code, penal code, code of civil procedure, code of penal procedure, and code of commerce. The civil code in Mexico is based on the French Napoleonic code in which suspects are considered guilty until proven innocent. Also, court judgments are based on laws rather than legal precedents.

Russia

In Russia, the most important laws are the constitutional laws taken from the constitution of the Russian Federation. The laws created by legislatures are called statutes, and they have a slightly inferior position. Russian law is divided into a series of codes. For example, business situations are governed by the Russian civil code. Decrees made by the president also acquire the force of law, but these decrees must not conflict with the constitution or with existing statutes.

Important terms

- Supranational: a governing body that joins multiple countries and gives each of them a vote; the United Nations and the European Union are both supranational organizations.
- National: a unified government that controls a territory and the citizens within it
- Regional: a government that organizes the people within a specific, geographically defined section of a larger nation
- Local: the government responsible for managing the smallest political unit in the larger country; in the United States, city and town governments are the most local.
- Plurality: Also known as the single-winner voting system or the proportional representation system, the winner is the candidate who receives the most votes.
- Simple majority: synonymous with plurality, meaning simply that the recipient of the most votes is the winner

- Absolute majority: To win, a candidate must receive more than half of all the votes cast. It can be difficult to achieve an absolute majority in a multiparty election, so there is typically a runoff system in place should a general election fail to produce a winner.
- Overall majority: the difference in votes between the first-place and second-place candidates in an election
- Runoff: a second election typically held after a primary in which no candidate receives an absolute majority. Runoff elections are generally restricted to the top two finishers in the previous election.
- Party system: the structure or organization of the political groups in a nation. The presence and arrangement of political parties determines the electoral and legislative processes in a state. Political parties tend to represent specific, though evolving, ideologies.
- One-party system: government controlled by a single political party. China has a one-party system because, though it is not the only party, the Communist Party dominates political life.
- Two-party system: a government dominated by representatives from two political parties. In the United States, the vast majority of political offices are held by Republicans or Democrats. These two parties vie to become the majority party. Systems in which only a simple majority is required for electoral victory tend to become dominated by two parties. When an absolute majority is required, it is more likely that smaller parties will survive.
- Judiciary: a country's court system. In most judiciaries, there is a supreme court at the top and a set of local courts at the bottom. There may also be military courts and courts of appeal.
- Autonomy of the judiciary: the court system's freedom from intervention by political officials or the military
- Judicial review: the process by which the courts evaluate, and occasionally strike down, actions taken by the executive or legislative branches; the courts are relied upon to verify the constitutionality of new laws or executive orders.
- Supreme Court: the highest court of appeals in most judicial systems. Most countries have supreme courts, as does the United Nations.

Citizens, Society, and the State

Political cleavage

Political cleavage is conflict or division within a political system, in particular when the division is caused by differences of race, religion, region, ethnicity, gender, or class. In democratic societies, all minority groups should have the opportunity to express their political will, so political cleavage should not lead to civil war. Those who feel their rights are being trampled can demonstrate, lobby, or file motions in court. However, when the country's constitution does not give citizens these options, violence and rebellion are more likely. Most political scientists look at political cleavage as a necessary and even a healthy consequence of diversity.

Ethnic political cleavages

Nigeria

There are three major ethnic groups in Nigeria: the Yoruba in the southwest, the Hausa-Fulani in the north, and the Igbo in the southeast. The conflict between these groups has continuously undermined the national government. In fact, after enduring persecution for perceived corruption, the Igbos attempted to separate from Nigeria in 1967. After three years of bloody violence, the Igbos relented and rejoined the country. Still, ethnic tensions simmer in present-day Nigeria.

Mexico

The large indigenous population in Mexico has long felt mistreated by the national government. In 1910, Mexico had a revolution that was ostensibly about improving life for peasants. Following the revolution, rural indigenous people received "ejidos," or small plots of land for shared farming. Unfortunately, these "ejidos" tended to be on rocky or unfertile soil, and the peasants were annoyed. Violence erupted in 1994 when an indigenous group called the Zapatistas revolted against the presence of American-owned factories (maquiladoras) in the state of Chiapas. Although the Zapatistas no longer advocate violence, they remain active in support of land reform and the rights of indigenous people.

Russian Federation

The Soviet monolith was, in fact, composed of many different ethnic groups, and after the breakup of the USSR, some of these groups demanded independence. In 1992, the Russian Federation (i.e., what remained of the USSR) signed the Federation Treaty with all of the territories under its control. Only Tatarland and Chechnya refused to sign this document. The Tatars eventually signed an agreement that gave them limited sovereignty, but the Chechens refused a similar treaty, and Chechen separatist groups continue to engage in sporadic violence. In 1993, a formal war was declared in Chechnya, but it ended with a peace treaty in 1997. A second armed conflict lasted from 1999, when Russian

Federation troops invaded Chechnya, until a decimated Chechen army basically surrendered in 2009.

<u>China</u>
In China, approximately 6 percent of the population is made up of ethnic minorities. The national government's response to ethnic cleavage has been alternately permissive and repressive. In part, this divided policy is the result of contradictory recommendations in the writings of Mao Zedong. Perhaps China's most important ethnic cleavage relates to what is technically a different country: Taiwan (though China does not recognize Taiwan's independence). China wants to formally reacquire Taiwan, but the United States and other nations back Taiwanese independence. China takes a more aggressive stance toward Tibet, which it annexed in the 1960s. The spiritual leader of Tibet, the Dalai Lama, has been forced into exile. Much of the Western world protests Chinese control of Tibet, but China shows little sign of relinquishing its control there.

Racial cleavage in Great Britain

There was a surge in immigration to Great Britain after World War II. Most of these immigrants were residents of former British colonies, and many of them were black. Great Britain's black population is only 3.8 percent of the total population, yet British police reported 47,000 racial incidents in 1999 and 2000. Since then, Britain has passed antiracism legislation and established a commission for racial equality. This commission has mounted a media campaign against racism and created support groups for victims of racism. Charges of racism in both government and private institutions are investigated seriously, and the commission is constantly on guard against "indirect racism," as for instance in education or literacy requirements for voting.

Class cleavage in Great Britain

Britain has traditionally been divided into three social groups: working class, middle class, and upper class. For a long time, political parties directly and explicitly appealed to the members of these classes, but now it is more common for a working-class citizen to be a member of the Conservative Party or for an upper-class citizen to join New Labour. This change has come about because the number of political parties in Great Britain has increased dramatically. In addition, and because many of these new parties focus on issues, like the environment, that are not specifically related to social class.

Gender cleavage

Iran

Iran's political system is characterized by significant gender cleavage, or the division between men and women. Women's rights have gradually expanded over the years, but most females in Iran still feel that they are treated as second-class citizens. In 2006, a coalition of Iranian women attempted to gather 1 million signatures on a petition to protest government discrimination against women. In particular, women in Iran would like to have more rights with respect to divorce and child custody proceedings. Currently, only a man can initiate a divorce in Iran. After the revolution of 1979, women could not be on the radio, and they could not sing on television. Also, women were forbidden from entering certain professions and from taking certain university classes. Although these policies were reversed because of their disastrous effects on the economy, Iranian women's rights still lag behind those of women in other Middle Eastern countries. However, Iranian women have received the right to vote and the right to hold any office besides the presidency.

Mexico

Mexico has a dispiriting history of gender cleavage. According to one shocking statistic, seven in ten Mexican women have been abused by their spouse. Hundreds of women have disappeared and are presumed murdered in the border city of Juarez. Although women have long been oppressed in Mexican culture, there has been a slow and steady shift toward gender equality. In the early 1960s, a group of upper-class women started a movement toward equal rights. In 1975, International Women's Year was celebrated in Mexico City, and the women's movement grew exponentially. Nevertheless, Mexican women are subject to lower pay and sexual harassment in the workplace. President Vicente Fox created the National Institute for Women. Fox's attorney general also created a special department to handle crimes committed against women.

Religious cleavage in Nigeria

In Nigeria, one of the direct effects of religious cleavage has been the imposition of sharia law in the north. This area of Nigeria is dominated by Muslims, and the central government has permitted the courts there to rule according to Islamic jurisprudence. For many Nigerians, this is a disheartening development, as they had thought the constitution of 1999 would implement a more progressive, Western-style judicial system. Indeed, the north's problems are not limited to legal issues. Religious cleavage has also contributed to infrastructure problems and continued violent conflict with Christians in the south.

Regional cleavage

<u>Russian Federation</u>
During the formation of the Russian Federation, both Tatarland and Chechnya sought independence. The Tatars eventually agreed to limited sovereignty, but Chechnya has continued to rebel against Russian control. Chechnya is a predominately Muslim region. Since the 1990s, there has been separatist violence in Chechnya, which Russia prizes for its oil reserves and its access to the Black Sea.

<u>Great Britain</u>
During the course of Great Britain's history, Northern Ireland, Scotland, and Wales have all tried to win independence from it. The British response has been devolution, or the assignment of limited rights to a territory or colony. In 1998, Great Britain's Parliament established the Scottish Parliament, Northern Ireland Assembly, and National Assembly for Wales. Regional issues are handled by these provincial legislatures. Each of these territories has nationalist political parties that run candidates for British Parliament, but few of their candidates have won. These parties exist mainly as a megaphone in London for local concerns, as the British Parliament continues to handle national issues.

Civil society

Civil society is the set of organizations in the nation that are not affiliated with any government office. The term *civil society* was coined by the eighteenth-century social philosopher Adam Ferguson. The participants in civil organizations are volunteers brought together by a shared interest. These groups have no legislative authority and are distinct from businesses. Some common examples of civil society organizations are unions, community organizations, and charities. Civil society organizations need not respect national boundaries, and they may operate throughout the world. Many of these groups are organized around a particular issue or cause.

<u>Nigeria</u>
In 2005, the CIVICUS Civil Society Index was implemented by ActionAid and DevNet, with the purpose of listing all the civil society organizations in Nigeria. It was thought that this project would enable leaders to strengthen the role of civil society and enable meaningful social change. Moreover, the very process of compiling the list encouraged the civil society organizations in Nigeria to communicate and collaborate with one another. Indeed, ActionAid and DevNet both report that more organizations have led active efforts for social reform in Nigeria in the years since the project was initiated.

China

As China has opened up in recent years, it has developed some elements of a civil society. For instance, there are now a few nongovernmental organizations (NGOs) that operate for the benefit of the Chinese people. These organizations are not affiliated with any political groups or government departments. In general, the development of a civil society is seen as a positive trend, as it is usually accompanied by the development of a more open and pluralistic society. In China, there is still some question about the distance between NGOs and the political apparatus. It is hard to avoid doing the bidding of the Communist Party in China, but organizations that support a particular political party are not considered to be part of a civil society. One notable example has been the development of organizations that deal with HIV and AIDS in China. Most observers see the development of a Chinese civil society as a hopeful sign, even though this emerging civil society is still a fragile one.

Iran

In Iran, every organization must abide by the strictures of Islam, the interpretation of which is left to the Iranian government. In 1997, the election of the relatively progressive President Mohammad Khatami spurred talks that Iran would develop a vibrant civil society. Conservatives there argue that the development of a civil society would be contrary to Islamic law, while some Iranian moderates argue that civil society could be fine as long as it is aligned with Islam. A third group, which seems to be representative of the majority opinion, asserts that civil society could do no harm and could help bring Iran into closer contact economically and diplomatically with the rest of the world.

Russian Federation

During the era of Vladimir Putin, many civil society organizations and nongovernmental organizations were marginalized or even eliminated. In 2009, a Freedom House report indicated that civil liberties have declined in Russia over the past three years. The government levies high registration fees on NGOs, which makes it difficult for new organizations to get off the ground. However, in January 2006, the Duma gave Russian citizens the right to vote on matters related to land use and civil planning. The government has even subsidized some citizen organizations and NGOs. The Siberian Civic Initiative Support Center was the first subsidized civil society organization in Russia, though its first funding came from the U.S. Agency for International Development (USAID). Since then, the role of civil organizations has increased in Russia. In 2006, 600 NGOs, including environmental groups, welfare rights organizations, and human rights campaigns, were given a grant of $15 million by the Russian Federation Public Chamber.

Mexico
In Mexico, as elsewhere, civil organizations work to solve social problems like land management, workers' rights, environmental preservation, and public health. In the past decade, a number of organizations have emerged to deal with the fallout from the development of American factories in the border areas of Mexico. One obstacle to the development of Mexican civil society has been continuous violence and drug wars, particularly near the northern border. Also, some civil organizations in Mexico have struggled with funding during an economic lull.

Media

There are all sorts of media outlets: radio, television, and newspapers, just to name a few. Many commentators distinguish between electronic and print media. Electronic media can deliver news almost instantaneously, while print media has an inevitable lag time. For this reason, publications like newspapers and magazines tend to provide a more detached, analytical overview of national events. The role of the news media is to convey important information to the general public so that voters can make good decisions and government activity can be scrutinized. People who work in the media have a responsibility to be accurate and fair, even when they have a partisan intent. News organizations usually make a distinction between straight reporting, which is intended to be an objective delivery of facts, and analysis, which permits the opinion of the journalist to emerge. In an authoritarian or totalitarian regime, there is no media independence, and certain views cannot be disseminated. Ideally, the media acts as a sort of watchdog on behalf of the public.

Iran
In Iran, the government exerts a great degree of control over the news media. Indeed, there are no private or independent news organizations in Iran. The information that citizens do receive from national news organizations tends to support the government's policies. Of course, in this era of global connectivity, it is impossible for the official media in Iran to go unchallenged. After Iran's 2009 election, many international media experts were very critical of the Iranian media's clear support for government-backed candidates. Notably, Iranians have long used illegal satellite dishes to obtain news from foreign services. The government has been unable to block access to the BBC, Voice of America, Radio France International, and Deutsche Welle.

Nigeria

In Nigeria, there is a large market for print media, and there are many successful newspapers and magazines. Although there are privately owned television and radio stations, the Nigerian government controls most of the electronic media. In many cases, the Nigerian media functions effectively, disseminating accurate information and supervising government activities. During the transition from military to democratic rule in 1998 and 1999, *Tell* magazine ran a weekly feature scrutinizing the handover of power. Since then, other publications have raised questions about campaign financing and corruption in the new government. As much as possible, the Nigerian media seeks to give equal coverage to the country's three major ethnic groups.

People's Republic of China

Since the Communists seized power in China, they have controlled all of the media. At times, the Communist Party has eased its grip on the media, only to tighten it again during times of insecurity. In the late 1970s, as China began to adopt some elements of a free-market system, government domination of the media was slightly diminished. Print and television commentators were allowed to express opinions about government policy as long as they did not directly subvert communist authority. However, there were crackdowns in 1983 and 1987, after which media outlets were required to receive permission from the Communist Party before publishing any potentially subversive material. After the Tiananmen Square massacre in 1989, many journalists were imprisoned or exiled. Since then, however, there has been gradual progress toward a free media, and it is possible these days for commentators to mildly criticize the government on air or in print.

Russia

In the heyday of the Soviet Union, magazines and newspapers were very cheap, so most citizens got their information from print media. Of course, the information the public received was vetted and edited by Communist Party officials and usually bore only a distant relationship to the truth. Part of Gorbachev's perestroika campaign was to diminish state influence on the media, but this meant removing much of the government funding, which bankrupted several news organizations. Those publications that survived had to restrict their reporting and publish fewer issues. After the fall of the Soviet Union, private investors began to take an interest in the media. In 1996, the Russian news media was heavily criticized for perceived bias in its coverage of the presidential elections. Many people charged that Russian newspapers and magazines largely existed as megaphones for the political views of their owners. These days, television is the dominant form of media in Russia, and virtually every household has at least one television. The government does not exercise any direct control over the content or programming of Russian television stations.

Mexico
During the seventy-plus years of the PRI party's rule in Mexico, the media was essentially monopolized by the Televisa group, which promoted the PRI party line. When PRI was finally defeated in the Mexican presidential election of 2000, other media organizations gained a foothold. These included foreign cable companies and the Azteca group. Mexican newspapers have been consistently popular, though they tend to focus on the sensational rather than the substantial. On a sad note, the watchdog organization Reporters Without Borders names Mexico the most deadly country for journalists because of the shockingly large number of assassinations of newspaper owners and investigative reporters.

Great Britain
In Great Britain, the media fulfills the normal functions of educating the public and scrutinizing the government. In a recent national election, Sky News hosted the first three televised debates in Britain's history. There were also televised debates for the financial officers of each major party. The editorial pages of British newspapers have particular power; their opinions and endorsements are very important to the electorate. When Britain holds an election, the BBC conducts voter interviews and exit polls, which help to clarify the reasons behind voting trends.

Political participation

Political participation refers to any activity that aims to influence the operations of the government. A general measure for the level of political participation in a society is the number of active citizens multiplied by their activities. Of course, this is only a crude measure of political participation. The most obvious form of political participation is membership and in support for a political party, though citizens may also participate politically by supporting interest groups, contacting elected officials, voting, and even running for office.

Iran
Although many people decry the theocratic regime in Iran, there was actually less political participation there before the revolution in 1979. During the reign of the shah, Iranian citizens had little confidence that their opinions or sentiments would be taken into account by government ministers. After the 1979 revolution, citizens found that they could participate in politics by working with religious institutions. There are Muslim organizations affiliated with schools and major employers, and these groups have excellent rates of political participation. Indeed, the blending of religious and political elements in Iranian culture has engendered relatively high levels of political participation, though many would argue that the capacity to create real change there is extremely small. Iranians who support the intermingling of religion and politics are called hezbollahs.

China
The total domination of the Communist Party in China severely limits political participation. In the past decade, however, some restrictions on citizen participation in government have been eased. At present, there are three types of organizations in which citizens can participate: the Communist Party, civic associations, and mass organizations. Even though the chances of creating significant change are small, Chinese people continue to participate in the political arena. For instance, the voting rate is high in China despite the fact that votes count for less there than they would in a democratic system. There are several organizations in China that sound as if they are political, but they are in fact apolitical. Some of these organizations include the Communist Youth League, which is a development program for aspiring party members; the All-China Women's Federation; and the All-China Federation of Trade Unions.

Nigeria
In Nigeria, a lack of political integration has diminished the amount of political participation. Nigerians tend to identify themselves as Igbo, Yoruba, or Hausa-Fulani rather than as Nigerian. There are also economic and religious divisions among Nigerians. The Igbos attempted to secede from Nigeria in 1967, and they remain skeptical about the national political scene. The difficulty of political participation in Nigeria was exemplified by the attempted census in the 1960s when each ethnic group tried to inflate its own numbers, resulting in violent riots. Moreover, the regular alternation of military and civilian governments has encouraged a pessimistic view of Nigerian politics, further decreasing political participation among citizens.

Mexico
Among Mexicans, participation in politics is directly proportionate to income: that is, upper-class Mexicans participate in politics to a much greater degree than do lower-class Mexicans. This is true in many countries, but it is especially so in Mexico, where the lower class is occupied entirely by the struggle for economic survival. Furthermore, there are relatively few aspects of the Mexican government that appeal to the lower class. In addition, there is a general perception that government officials are susceptible to bribes, which further cements the idea that only money can make political participation worthwhile.

Great Britain
In Great Britain, there has recently been a steady decline in political participation. The ever-increasing duties of a Parliament member have discouraged many people from seeking office. Members of Parliament (MPs) must constantly commute between their home district and the House of Commons, and they must maintain a high level of knowledge on important political subjects. Nevertheless, MPs are almost always required to vote with their parties, and there is very little chance for a member to develop his own identity in Parliament. Since 1964, the voting rate in Great Britain has dropped by 18 percent, namely because of

cynicism among young people. Some critics charge that the news media is responsible for increasing skepticism among voters about government's efficacy. To fight against this prevailing notion, the British government has developed promotional campaigns for television and the Internet.

Political violence

Political violence is considered to be an example of political participation only when it is performed by citizens. Violence used by the state to maintain control or suppress rebellion does not count as political participation. Throughout history, citizens have used violent rebellion, protest, and terrorism to force change in their society. In most cases, political violence is performed by the members of a minority or marginal group. It is more common in societies where the normal avenues for political participation have been closed off.

Russia in 1917

In 1917, the simmering conflict between landowners and peasants was finally resolved by violent revolution. Russia's czar had made well-intentioned but unsuccessful attempts to raise the quality of life for peasants. Indeed, in 1861, the serfs were emancipated. However, there was never any satisfactory resolution of the landownership question, and in 1905, there were numerous peasant rebellions that had to be violently repressed by the royal government. The czar attempted to resolve the situation by allowing poor peasants to sell their land to the rich, but this only exacerbated disparities among the newly integrated serfs. By the time of the revolution in 1917, only one in ten peasant families owned the land on which they lived. Consequently, at the same time that the Bolsheviks were overthrowing the czar in St. Petersburg, the peasants were rebelling against their landowners in the countryside.

Social movements

Social movements are collections of people who organize themselves with the intent of creating political change. Activities like meetings, petitions, rallies, and campaigns are typical of social movements. In most cases, social movements are in support of groups who feel marginalized or repressed by the government or by society at large. Some of the more famous social movements in the United States have been those related to women's rights, the environment, civil rights, and gay rights. Social movements usually arise in the cities because greater population density makes it easier for people to organize and gather together.

As categorized by social and political scientists, social movements are:

- Reform movements: social movements aimed at changing social and political norms. Some common examples are the movements to abolish capital punishment and abortion.
- Radical movements: social movements intended to change the fundamental values of a society, not just opinions on certain issues. The civil rights movement and the Polish solidarity movement, which was against the communist government there, were both radical movements.
- Innovation movements: social movements aimed at implementing new solutions, such as nuclear power or the Internet
- Conservative movements: social movements concentrated on maintaining current policies and norms. Some conservative causes include opposition to gay marriage and reduction of the federal income tax.
- Group-focused movements: social movements aimed at changing a particular group, whether it be a political party or a smaller faction
- Individual-focused movements: social movements that emphasize personal change. Religious and self-help movements, for example, are focused on the individual.
- Peaceful movements: social movements focused on using nonviolent means to achieve their ends. One recent example of a peaceful movement was the civil rights movement.
- Violent movements: social movements ready to use violence and terrorism to achieve their goals. Militant Islamists constitute a violent movement.
- Old movements: social movements that began in the nineteenth century or earlier. The old movements that remain are largely concerned with improving conditions for a certain group, such as workers or women.
- New movements: social movements that originated after 1950. Some of the more famous new movements are feminism, environmentalism, and the civil right movement.
- Global movements: social movements focused on creating worldwide change, particularly with respect to the environment
- Local movements: social movements concentrated on making changes at a community level. Local movements are often concerned with parochial issues like water rights or land preservation.
- Multilevel movements: social movements aimed at change on the local, regional, national, and international levels

Social representation and citizenship

Social representation theory asserts that the members of a group will develop a unique understanding of certain concepts related to the group's activities. For instance, members of a group often develop a new vocabulary to describe their work. Political scientists propose that this phenomenon is the result of a desire to have something unique in common with comrades and to differentiate the members of the group from society at large. By using the code, group members signify their loyalty and ingratiate themselves to one another. Citizenship, meanwhile, is official membership in a social group, political party, or country. Citizenship often entails certain responsibilities, such as paying taxes or performing community service. In the past few decades, citizens for the first time have become members of supranational organizations like the European Union. It is possible to be a citizen of several different entities at the same time.

Serge Moscovici
Serge Moscovici is credited with coining the phrase "social representation" to describe the behavior of the members of specialized groups. His study focused on three social groups in France during the 1950s: communists, Catholics, and urban liberals. Moscovici examined the responses of these three groups to the theory of psychoanalysis. Communists largely had a negative response and used propaganda to disseminate their views on the subject. Catholics had a moderately accepting view of psychoanalysis. They tended to use "propagation," or a means of aligning a new set of ideas with existing tenets of the group. In this case, that meant making psychoanalysis compatible with Catholic doctrine. Finally, urban liberals were very receptive to psychoanalysis and used "diffusion" to declare their enthusiasm. Moscovici identified two ways that social groups deal with new information: "objectification," in which an abstract concept is converted into a more tangible form, and "anchoring," in which a concept is explicitly related to existing group ideas.

Political and Economic Change

Revolution, coup, and war

A revolution is the overthrow, usually by violence, of a particular regime or government. To be successful, a revolution usually needs the support of the majority of the population or at least the majority of the most important elements of the population. Also, a revolution typically has explicit goals for what it will do when it achieves power. A coup, or coup d'état, is the rapid overthrow of a regime by some element within the country, usually the military. In some cases, violence is not even necessary to carry out a coup d'état. Regimes may also be overthrown by war, particularly civil war.

Military coups in Nigeria

After Nigeria received independence from Great Britain in 1960, it established a parliamentary system of government quite similar to the British model. Unfortunately, the Nigerian version was quickly overwhelmed by corruption, and the government was taken over by the military in 1966. After thirteen years of relatively stable military rule, Nigeria again tried to implement a constitutional system. However, there were frequent and widespread complaints of election fraud, and the military intervened again in 1983. From 1985 to 1993, Nigeria was controlled by General Ibrahim Babangida. Under his rule, the capital was moved to a neutral location, former officeholders were forbidden from reentering politics, and only two political parties were allowed. Babangida was ousted by General Sani Abacha in 1993. Six years later, Nigeria crafted yet another constitution, this time modeled after that of the United States. The resulting government has survived, though just barely.

Political change

Mexico
Several factors contributed to the downfall of the PRI party in Mexico's 2000 election. Perhaps the main reason for PRI's defeat, however, was that the public had grown weary of the corruption and information control the party routinely used to maintain its dominance. PRI officials were notorious for pandering to wealthy donors and important groups in Mexican society. The public grew tired of seeing each successive PRI president retire inexplicably wealthy. Also, the public began to resent the system of "dedazo," whereby the PRI president would anoint his successor. In 1976, the PAN party had even declined to take part in elections, at which point the PRI made some slight changes to bolster the appearance of democracy. Other political parties were guaranteed seats in parliament, and they used these positions to mount a serious critique of PRI.

72

Many observers of Mexico content that PRI's decline began after its response to PAN's refusal to take part in the 1979 elections. At that time, PAN was associated with conservative institutions like the business community and the Catholic Church. PAN declined to participate in elections because the party claimed it was really in favor of PRI. This generated unwelcome attention to Mexico's corrupt politics, and PRI was forced to make certain concessions, like guaranteeing seats in the Chamber of Deputies for members of opposition parties. This opened the door for PAN and other parties to gain influence, and PAN candidates won numerous gubernatorial races in northern Mexico. Finally, PAN candidate Vicente Fox was elected president of Mexico in 2000.

After the PRI party's stranglehold on Mexican politics was broken in 2000, the Mexican legislature became more representative of the entire society. The traditions of political patronage and election fraud were eliminated, though bribery in government has been more difficult to eradicate. Also, Mexican politics continues to be rife with "camarillas," which are shadowy political groups devoted to advancing the careers of particular individuals. Many people still feel that it is impossible to succeed in Mexican politics without having connections at the highest levels. Resentment of the government is especially strong among the indigenous peoples in impoverished regions like Chiapas. Nevertheless, most observers agree that Mexico's political system has made significant progress in the past decade.

Iran

One of several factors that led to the overthrow of the shah in 1979 was the public's antipathy toward the harsh methods of his regime. The shah also behaved inappropriately, which many religious Iranians found offensive. Much of the country was deeply impoverished, and many people felt that Iranian oil wealth should be distributed more fairly. In addition to all of these factors, the Iranian public disapproved of the shah's close relationship with the United States. The American government gave financial and other support to the shah because he was considered a bulwark against communism in the region. However, critics of this relationship alleged that American influence was infecting Iranian society with Western vices like alcoholism. Taken together, these factors promoted the overthrow of the shah in the late 1970s.

The current regime in Iran came to power after the overthrow of Shah Reza Pahlavi in 1978 and 1979. Most Iranians disapproved of the shah not only for his harsh repression of citizens, but also for his close alliance with the United States. A group of influential clerics mounted a rebellion against the shah and the society he had created. These clerics were outraged by the advances of Western habits like alcohol consumption and public displays of affection. The leader of the clerics, Ayatollah Khomeini, returned after the overthrow of the shah and helped develop a constitution that made Iran an Islamic state.

Despite the many faults of Iran's current regime, most Iranians probably prefer it to the brutal and exploitative era of the shah. Still, the theocracy now in charge does not allow dissent and is in no way democratic. After seizing power in 1979, one of the first acts of the new regime was to hold employees at the American embassy in Iran hostage for more than a year. A few years later, Ayatollah Khomeini issued a fatwa, or death warrant, against the writer Salman Rushdie, who had made comments perceived as hostile to Islam in his book *The Satanic Verses*. Even now, though Iran attempts to portray itself as a democratic country, it continues to be governed in reality by a small group of clerics.

Russia
The Russian Federation was the product of several important factors: forced agricultural collectivization, communist repression, disastrous five-year industrial plans, and a shift toward reform during the years of Mikhail Gorbachev. The Soviet Union existed from roughly 1917 to 1989, during which time the authoritarian government forced peasants to organize their land into collectives. These collectives were incredibly inefficient, and millions of Russians starved to death. In the cities, chaotic bureaucracies made it impossible for factory managers to meet their production targets. Gorbachev's campaign of perestroika aimed to reform Russian industry, but instead it exposed the override that had developed in Soviet infrastructure and management. At the same time, Gorbachev was spearheading a campaign of glasnost, which was to liberate the news media. However, many of the empowered commentators were critical of Gorbachev, which severely weakened his government.

By the end of the 1980s, there was almost universal dissatisfaction with the Soviet Union's communist government. Although Mikhail Gorbachev did not wish to destroy the Communist Party, he knew it needed to be reformed. His campaigns of perestroika and glasnost were meant to give more autonomy to factory managers and the media, respectively, but these policies ended up backfiring by exposing inefficiencies and corruption in the Soviet bureaucracy. For the Soviet people, then, Gorbachev's reforms produced little in the way of results. As the government opened itself up and became a bit more transparent, it only incited calls for more complete democracy. In 1991, a candidate unaffiliated with the Communist Party, Boris Yeltsin, was elected president of the Russian Soviet Republic. By Christmas of 1991, the former Soviet Union was a thing of the past. By 1992, the Communist Party had fallen out of power in Russia.

Upon his election as president of Russia, Boris Yeltsin immediately made some significant changes. Parts of the former Soviet Union had declared their independence, and Yeltsin renamed the remaining country the Russian Federation. In 1993, a new constitution was drafted, which gave the Russian president the authority to rule by decree during national emergencies, call for new elections whenever he liked, and dissolve the legislature. The constitution was approved by popular vote. Yeltsin used military force to suppress a nascent rebellion by legislators. The Russian Federation's entry into the international market was rocky, with persistent corruption and high inflation.

Nigeria

In the 1960s and 1970s, several factors inhibited political stability in Nigeria: a lack of nationalism, a diverse population, and the unfortunate traditions of the "dash" (bribery) and the "chop" (ethnic favoritism). In 1966, the Nigerian government tried to take a census and instead had to quell riots after each ethnic group attempted to artificially inflate its own numbers. Several times in Nigeria's history, the military has had to intervene and maintain stability until a civilian government could be formed.

Many Nigerians welcomed military rule because they thought it would bring stability. However, after the military officer Ironsi declared that Nigeria would become a unitary system, there was widespread fear that one ethnic group, the Igbos, would dominate. Violent protests were launched, Ironsi was killed, and the Igbos attempted to secede from the country. A few years later, in 1979, General Olusegun Obasanjo restored democracy in Nigeria. The country's new constitution was modeled after that of the United States, but the system soon failed and the military took over again. This time, General Ibrahim Babangida tried to make specific changes to prepare the nation for democracy: he limited the number of political parties, redrew the state's boundaries, and moved the capital to an area free from ethnic tension. However, Babangida was replaced by General Sani Abacha. Over the next five years, Abacha's reign of terror undid many of the positive changes instituted by Babangida. Most recently, Nigeria's 1999 constitution established a tenuous democracy.

There are all sorts of factors conspiring against democracy in Nigeria: election fraud, poverty, corruption, and a lack of nationalism are just a few. Many Nigerians are more loyal to their ethnic group or religious group than to the nation. This is one reason why Nigeria has had a hard time building and sustaining a British-style parliamentary system and subsequently an American-style federal system. Nigerians are extremely skeptical of what they see as a corrupt government, and many of them are so preoccupied with the struggle to escape poverty that they have no time for politics. For many Nigerians, the days of military rule were a time of welcome stability.

China

War and the mobilization of the peasants were major factors in China's turn to communism. Before the Communists took over, they had to struggle for more than two decades against the nationalist forces led by Chiang Kai-shek. Nationalists were not defeated until 1949. One of the reasons for the success of the Communists was the popularity of the "mass line" idea propagated by Mao Zedong. In part, this was a conscious decision to focus not on communist theory, but on the improvement of life in the country. Mao led campaigns to build dams, improve infrastructure, and help with the harvest. Peasants appreciated these efforts and lent their support to the Communists.

During the 1980s and 1990s there were many factors that inhibited efforts to make communist China more democratic. The Chinese communist regime's handling of dissent has in some ways contributed to the trend toward openness over the past decade. China's government has varied its approach to dissidents, alternating between permissiveness and repression. One example was the establishment of the Democracy Wall in Beijing in 1979 by student Wei Jiangsheng. This wall was covered with posters advocating a Fifth Modernization, which would follow the Four Modernizations of Deng Xiaoping. The previous modernizations were economic; however, this modernization would be political, moving the country toward democracy. Although the Democracy Wall was permitted to exist for a few months, it was eventually taken down, and Wei was imprisoned. Another example of China's varied attitude toward dissidents was the Tiananmen Square massacre in June 1989. After debating what to do at great length, the Communist Party ultimately decided on harsh repression, and approximately 1,400 dissident students were killed. The massacre deterred other Chinese citizens from protesting for democracy.

The Chinese government's violent response to the protests in Tiananmen Square had significant political consequences. The Chinese government was heavily criticized by other countries and by human rights organizations. Within the country, dissident groups decided that the Chinese government would no longer tolerate any form of criticism. At the same time, the crackdown demonstrated the Chinese government's ability to control its workforce. After the massacre, China's already restrictive media policy became even more so. Although the United Nations strongly condemned the crackdown on protesters, it was forbidden by its charter from interfering with internal matters in a sovereign nation. One punishment exacted by the international community was the cancellation of all loans to China by the EU. Even today, the EU has an arms embargo against China.

European Union
The formation of the European Union began with the Treaty of Rome in 1957. This agreement created a shared market in Europe, with regulations on the production and taxation of coal and steel. The Treaty of Rome was signed by West Germany, Italy, France, Belgium, Luxembourg, and Holland. Over the years, the coalition gained members, and in 1995, there were fifteen signatories to the treaty. In 1991, the Maastricht treaty established a common currency: the euro. In 2001, an attempt was made to draft an EU constitution, but it was ultimately defeated by Holland and France. Finally, in 2009, the EU member nations agreed on a constitution, known as the Treaty of Lisbon, despite some concerns that increasing the power of this supranational organization would diminish the national identity of each of its respective members.

One of the main reasons why some European countries are resistant to joining the EU is that they fear a loss of their culture and national identity. EU membership means abiding by the constitution; taking part in the EU's judicial system; and, for many countries, adopting a new currency. Great Britain is an example of a country that has retained its original currency because of its feelings of patriotism. Some countries wanted to join the EU but were prevented from doing so because they could not meet the convergence criteria (basic financial stability tests). Even now, member countries like Greece are struggling to maintain financial stability, and the other EU nations are cooperating to ensure that Greek problems do not infect the rest of the organization.

Great Britain
As prime minister, Margaret Thatcher brought an aggressive and sometimes controversial brand of conservatism to British politics. She was extremely critical of the powerful labor unions, which she believed were responsible for the decline in British industry. In 1984 and 1985, she won a series of victories over striking coal miners, which greatly improved her standing relative to the unions. Thatcher went on to privatize important British interests like British Airways, British Petroleum, and Rolls Royce. She also sold off thousands of government-owned council homes that had been functioning as low-cost housing for poor people. Although Thatcher was credited with expanding the British economy, her programs also increased inflation, unemployment, taxation, and homelessness.

Economic growth

When an economy produces more, it is said to be growing. Economic growth may be caused by increases in innovation, land, labor, and capital. It may be the result of technological advances or the greater availability of natural resources. However, economists agree that it is very difficult to sustain economic growth without well-defined property rights, enforceable contracts, and a stable government. Also, sustained economic growth typically requires a well-educated and large workforce.

Economic change

Mexico
In recent years, the Mexican economy has been bolstered by the government's infrastructure improvements to airports, railroads, and seaports. The North American Free Trade Agreement (NAFTA), which was signed in 1994 by Mexico, the United States, and Canada, has brought many factory jobs to northern Mexico, where the cost of labor is lower. Furthermore, Mexico has become a significant producer of oil, much of which is sold to the United States.

Nigeria

In Nigeria, inflation has severely damaged the economy since the establishment of the present government in 1999. Indeed, the 2005 inflation rate was approximately 15.6 percent, which means that Nigerian workers were getting much less for their money than they had in the past. The gross domestic product of Nigeria is lower than it was when Nigeria won its independence in 1960. Over 50 percent of the Nigerian population earns less than a dollar a day, and the Nigerian government's tax revenues are small because of poverty and inefficient bureaucracies. Nigeria is currently running a budget deficit. It used to be a major exporter of palm oil, rubber, peanuts, and cocoa; however, agricultural problems have diminished the nation's capacity. There is also a serious epidemic of hunger in Nigeria. Finally, oil companies have exploited indigenous people in rural Nigeria, exacerbating poverty and creating lawlessness.

China

Mao's Great Leap Forward, a fifteen-year plan for transitioning China from an agricultural economy to an industrial economy, only lasted two disastrous years. Part of the plan was to produce "backyard steel," which required thousands of trees to be cut down so that the iron ore could be smelted. The erosion caused by this process left the Chinese countryside vulnerable to devastating floods. At the same time, the government's encouragement for peasants to work on communes was met with much resistance, and agricultural production declined as a result. This problem was compounded by the mass migration of farmworkers to the growing cities. In 1961 and 1962, China endured a terrible famine.

Soviet Union

Joseph Stalin implemented a series of five-year plans designed to industrialize the Soviet Union. Part of this effort involved collectivizing farms so that more people could move to the cities and work in factories. However, Stalin determined that one ethnic group, the kulaks, would never agree to this arrangement, so he had them all killed. Disorganization and a scarcity of laborers led to massive famines throughout the Soviet Union. It is believed that 10 million people died of starvation in the Ukraine alone. At the same time, the factories struggled to produce goods at the unreasonable rates demanded by communist officials. Corruption and mismanagement in factories became commonplace, and the quality of Soviet goods quickly declined.

Russian Federation

It was not easy for the new Russian Federation to privatize virtually the entire economy. After the Soviet Union fell, the Russian Federation's new president, Boris Yeltsin, undertook a major reform campaign to introduce the nation to the free market. At first, it was quite unsuccessful, and a group of organized criminals tied to government officials became very wealthy by illegal means. This group was known as the "nomenklatura." Yeltsin's efforts to enter international markets also failed, and excessive attention to currency rates resulted in inflation. In

1998, the plummeting value of the ruble (the Russian Federation's currency) combined with widespread public skepticism sent the Russian economy into crisis. Over the next decade, however, the nation was able to gain its footing, the ruble stabilized, foreign investment increased, and Russia became a major exporter of oil and gas.

<u>Mexico</u>
Since signing the North Atlantic Free Trade Agreement (NAFTA), Mexico's export levels have risen by five times. However, the American-owned factories that were built in northern Mexico tended to use American parts suppliers, which bankrupted many Mexican firms. Also, Mexican farmers struggled to compete with large-scale growers to the north, who were now able to compete in the Mexican market because of the elimination of tariffs. After thriving for a few years, the Mexican technology industry has lost considerable ground to China, which can offer even lower production costs to manufacturers. Mexico's auto manufacturers have struggled almost as much as American ones. Although NAFTA has brought some economic growth to Mexico, it has not solved all of Mexico's problems, which is why immigration from Mexico to the United States continues at a steady pace.

Privatization

Privatization is the sale of formerly government-run operations to nongovernment interests. For example, a government might decide to sell the rights to the water or telephone service because it believes a private entity will serve the public better. Supporters of capitalism believe that the demands of the free market force businesses to improve. Conversely, an industry whose existence is guaranteed by the government will have little incentive to innovate. Nevertheless, many people feel that some specific industries, such as schools and prisons, should be run by the government and protected from market turbulence.

Relationship between political and economic change

In many—if not most—cases, there are economic reasons for political change. When people are poor, when inflation is high, and when jobs are scarce, politicians are likely to bear the brunt of citizen outrage. This outrage can lead to regime change in the form of an election or even a violent rebellion. The government that emerges from the regime change will have to take immediate and wide-reaching economic action. If inflation can be controlled and foreign investment can be corralled, the government can get away with temporarily nationalizing some of the country's industries.

Globalization

Globalization is a multiform process that occurs anytime businesses and governments make international deals, establish tariffs or quotas, or exchange economic information. The primary engine of globalization in Europe is the European Union, which has eliminated tariffs between member countries. Corporations also contribute to globalization insofar as they often have offices or factories in many different countries. The trend toward globalization has increased the size of the market for exporters. The globalization process has been further aided by global groups like the World Trade Organization. One consequence of globalization is that manufacturing jobs have been sent to countries in which workers earn relatively low wages.

Opponents of globalization dislike what they see as the inordinate political influence of multinational corporations. According to globalization critics, corporations are allowed to manipulate financial markets and exploit poor people. These critics cite unfair labor agreements in developing countries as evidence of the evil of globalization. Also, when accidents happen in the workplace, globalization opponents are quick to point to lax safety regulations and standards in many nations. Finally, critics charge that globalization is bad for the environment because corporations can choose to manufacture goods in the countries with the most relaxed pollution controls.

Fragmentation, interlinked economies, global culture, and regionalism

Fragmentation is a weakening in the bonds between the members of the global community. In some cases, this fragmentation can lead to the dissolution of a country, an economy, a global industry, or a supranational organization. When economies are interlinked, they cooperate with one another and share information related to manufacturing and the provision of services. A global culture has developed as nations have been brought into closer economic contact with one another. Today, there is a high degree of interdependency in the global economy; this interdependency strengthens and ultimately solidifies a global culture. Finally, regionalism is allegiance to a particular part of a country rather than to the country in its entirety.

Public Policy

Effects of public policy on economic performance

Nigeria
Beginning in 2003, the Nigerian National Economic Empowerment Development Strategy (NEEDS) attempted to remedy some of the nation's basic infrastructure problems. In particular, this program tried to deliver fresh water, provide consistent electricity, and construct safe roads. Also, NEEDS aimed to reduce government corruption and create 7 million new jobs. Another public policy program in Nigeria, sponsored by the United Nations, is the National Millennium Goals for Nigeria. This program began in 2000 and is slated to last fifteen years. Its goal is to improve education and health and to reduce poverty. Although Nigeria had not been able by 2004 to reduce poverty, AIDS, or maternal mortality, the National Millennium Goals for Nigeria program is considered a success because it has improved education, environmental awareness, and global development. Government corruption, however, continues to bedevil Nigerian public policy efforts.

Mexico
The Mexican government has succeeded at gradually expanding the nation's gross domestic product. In 2009, Mexico's GDP was endangered by a brief credit crisis, though this has largely passed. The Mexican government has tried to stabilize the economy by lowering energy prices and by subsidizing the construction of roads, oil wells, and railways. Mexico also provides health care and part-time jobs to unemployed citizens. The value of the peso (the Mexican currency) is much more stable than it used to be. The Mexican government also offers loans to small businesses. In the coming years, Mexican government officials hope to improve working conditions and edit the tax code.

China
In China, gradual economic reform has been taking place since December 1978. These efforts have been aimed at modernizing and liberating the state-controlled economy. Although the socialist command economy and the Great Leap Forward were extremely unsuccessful, the reform of the past few decades has succeeded. Indeed, high production levels in both industry and agriculture have improved the quality of life for all levels of citizens. Under Mao, the poverty level was 53 percent, but it had improved to 19 percent by 1985 and fell to only 6 percent by 2001. Moreover, by 2005, over 70 percent of the country's gross domestic product was in the private sector. In the public sector, which consists of 200 massive state-run operations, bureaucratic efficiency programs have increased productivity as well. Despite all these changes, China continues to define itself as a socialist nation.

Soviet Russia
Even just a few years after the revolution of 1917, Vladimir Lenin's New Economic Policy mingled private enterprise with state-run industry. Farmers had to produce a certain amount of crops for the government, but they were free to sell the rest on their own crops. Joseph Stalin continued this policy, believing that it would help Russia gain international leverage. Although the New Economic Policy increased agricultural production, state-run factories descended into mismanagement and incompetence. Manufacturers raised prices to offset low production, and the value of the ruble declined as a result. The simultaneous rise in the price of industrial goods and decline in the price of agricultural goods is known historically as the "scissor crisis." In 1928, Stalin terminated the New Economic Policy and implemented the first of many five-year plans.

Effects of public policy on social welfare

Great Britain
Great Britain is referred to as a welfare state because it guarantees a minimum income and health care for all its citizens. Despite this guarantee, however, the British government does not always provide essential services, particularly in health care, where long waits and bureaucratic inefficiencies have been problematic. In the 1960s and 1970s, the British government tried to reform the healthcare system by giving control of expenditures to the Treasury. In the 1980s and 1990s, large administrative departments were broken up into smaller agencies as a means of increasing efficiency. More recently, some British government agencies have been privatized in the hopes of improving their performance.

European Union
All of the European Union's member nations have signed a Charter of Fundamental Rights, which guarantees universal health care and equal pay for equal work and which outlaws capital punishment. The 2009 EU constitution includes measures that allow member nations to cooperate on initiatives to improve the health of their citizens. To this end, states are charged with defining health policies and allocating certain amounts of money to support these programs. Some of the new items in the EU constitution oppose discrimination, guarantee employment and education, and support animal welfare.

China
In the People's Republic of China, the Ministry of Human Resources and Social Security is responsible for social welfare issues. Through the 1980s, all the social welfare needs of the Chinese population were met by the socialist state. Certain responsibilities were assigned to industries run by the government. For instance, employment, health care, child care, housing, and care for the elderly were all handled by employers, a system known as the "iron rice bowl." The modernization of Chinese industry has altered this social welfare approach in

recent years. For example, in the 1990s, social welfare reforms were enacted to handle pension funds, medical insurance, and unemployment insurance.

Public policy and civil liberties

Iran
Although Iran claims to be an industrial democracy, it is in reality a fundamentalist Islamic theocracy. There is no free speech in Iran, and those who are merely suspected of dissidence can be arrested and tortured. Iranian law is based on sharia, or Islamic law. The rights of women in Iran are complicated. Women must obey strict Islamic codes related to behavior and dress, and women have no right to protection from domestic violence under Iranian law. Nevertheless, women are allowed to run for public office. Citizens are not allowed to protest the Iranian government, as evidenced by the harsh suppression of protesters after the 2009 election. The Iranian government also attempts to censor the Internet and prevent citizens from accessing foreign media sources, though it is not entirely successful in this effort.

Nigeria
In May 1999, the military government of Nigeria peacefully made way for a new constitution. This constitution contained a bill of rights, which established a strong set of civil liberties for Nigerian citizens. Nigerians are guaranteed the rights to liberty, life, dignity, privacy, and a fair hearing in court. They are also guaranteed the freedoms of thought, religion, expression, the press, movement, and property. Finally, Nigerians are guaranteed freedom from discrimination. So far, the Nigerian government has only been somewhat successful in enforcing these rights.

China
China draws frequent and loud criticism for its civil liberties abuses. Critics of the Chinese nation point to the Tiananmen Square massacre, capital punishment, the handling of Tibet, and the repressive one-child policy as examples of inhumane government practice. Also, China severely limits freedom of speech and freedom of the press. Dissidents are often arrested and held without formal charges for years. China's poor human rights record has only become more evident as more citizens have moved to the cities. Currently, citizens in the burgeoning and more progressive cities are granted greater civil liberties than are peasants in the countryside.

Public policy and environmental issues

Russia
Historically, the Soviet Union paid almost no attention to environmental issues because its leaders felt that the natural resources of the large nation were essentially limitless. This laissez-faire attitude resulted in approximately 40 percent of Russia's land being environmentally stressed by the 1990s. In 1986, there was a major disaster at the Russian nuclear power station at Chernobyl. Around the same time, the Aral Sea began to dry up, and the presence of harmful radiation was detected at the Semey nuclear test site. Widespread use of leaded fuel in Russian cars continues to create air pollution problems in the cities, which has contributed to poor health for many citizens. Finally, with the advent of the Russian Federation, the first piece of environmental legislation was passed in 1991. It was called On Environmental Protection, and though it meant well, the wording was too vague to be very useful.

Nigeria
During the twentieth century, Nigeria's tenuous and often short-lived governments paid little attention to the environment. As a result, deforestation, desertification, harmful agricultural practices, and the unchecked growth of cities wreaked havoc on Nigeria's natural resources. In 1987, the Nigerian government issued the Harmful Wastes decree, the nation's first effort at environmental regulation. In 1988, the Nigerian government created the Federal Environmental Protection Agency. Four years later, the Nigerian government issued a decree requiring businesses and government agencies to compose an environmental impact assessment before initiating any program. At the same time, Nigeria has vastly improved the regulation of its oil industry. However, the bureaucratic inefficiencies that plague all aspects of Nigerian government can also be found in Nigerian environmental regulation.

China
One of the biggest environmental problems in China is soil pollution, and no laws have been passed to handle this problem to date. Nevertheless, the Chinese government performed a comprehensive survey of soil pollution levels in 2006. The survey determined the levels of heavy metals, organic pollutants, and pesticides in the soil. The main culprits of this pollution are industrial and agricultural waste. It is estimated that 20 percent of the arable land in China is polluted. This problem is not easily solved and requires more than simply abandoning the destructive practices of the past. Although the Chinese government has acknowledged the necessity of dealing with soil pollution problems, it has not moved quickly in doing so.

Public policy and economic development

Nigeria
In Nigeria, the economy is overly focused on petroleum at the expense of all other industries. Since the passage of the constitution in 1999, the Nigerian government has moved to create a more market-based economy by privatizing the national oil industry. Against the regulations of the World Trade Organization, Nigeria has banned many different imports so as to protect domestic producers. However, in recent years, Nigeria has begun to allow some textiles to be imported, and the overall number of banned imports has decreased. Nigeria has also created a government commission to handle intellectual property violations, and a national anticorruption law has been passed, though it requires the support of all thirty-six Nigerian states to work.

Mexico
The Mexican government offers subsidies to domestic industry and tax breaks for start-up businesses. The 1917 constitution encouraged government ownership of industry, and in that spirit, the government took over the railroads, banks, electric companies, and even the Mexican holdings of foreign oil companies in 1938. In the 1970s, the government's focus was on improving agricultural production, expanding the fishing industry, and improving the railroad system. One mistake that the Mexican government made was overinvesting in the oil industry; when oil prices plummeted during the 1980s, there was a financial crisis in Mexico. In 1989, the Mexican government began to privatize industries, including the banks, airlines, telephone company, copper mines, and steel companies. Since this wave of privatization, the Mexican economy has been much more turbulent.

China
In 1949, Communists took control of both the Chinese government and the Chinese economy. There was an immediate initiative for land reform in the country. At the same time, the government nationalized finance, communications, energy, railways, and other industries. Positive consequences of the communist takeover were the termination of opium production and the subsequent decline in opium addiction. The government implemented a new currency and was able to stop the inflation trend that had been causing problems during the late 1940s. According to the World Bank, China's economy grew steadily from 1949 to 1978, at which point it began to gradually transition from a planned economy to a market economy. Although the government retains tight control of Chinese industry, foreign trade and investment are now welcomed. This process of opening up has only increased the growth of China's economy.

Domestic factors influencing public policy

The domestic organization in a country largely determines its public policy. Some of the domestic factors that are most influential in public policymaking and implementation are constituents, special interest groups, fiscal events, political ideology, and the media. The legislators in a country always have to respect the wishes of their constituents lest they be voted out of office. A country must also take into account whether it is in debt or running a surplus. A country that is deeply in debt cannot afford expensive public policies. The political ideology of the party in power usually has a great deal to do with the public policy measures that are promoted and passed. Finally, the positivity or negativity of media coverage for a policy proposal will have a significant effect on a particular policy's success.

International factors influencing public policy

Public policy can also be influenced by international factors. For instance, economic treaties will adjust the incentives for various public policy actions. They will also determine the extent to which a country regulates its imports, exports, and tariffs. Many nations have military treaties as well. For instance, the United States has declared that it will support Taiwan should the island nation be invaded by China. In some countries, political instability leads to inaction. One example would be Nigeria before 1999; uncertainty about the military government made it difficult for the nation to engage in international trade. Some nations, like Iran, become pariahs internationally and have a hard time cooperating on trade agreements for that reason. Finally, many nations decide public policy issues based on their perceived effects on the value of that nation's own currency relative to the currencies of other nations.

Practice Test

1. Which country executes more people?
    a. Great Britain
    b. Mexico
    c. Russia
    d. China
    e. Nigeria

2. The European Union's first treaties focused on building:
    a. A common market
    b. Environmental stability
    c. Humanitarian values
    d. Peace and stability
    e. Solidarity

3. Private ownership of what is controversial in Russia?
    a. Goods
    b. Investments
    c. Land
    d. Businesses
    e. Technology

4. The tax collection problem in Russia is caused by what?
    a. Confusing policies and poorly trained officials
    b. High natural resource taxes
    c. High income taxes
    d. An inaccurate census and new tax policies
    e. Corruption, tax evasion, and lack of cooperation by local officials

5. Which is the oldest liberal democracy?
    a. Iran
    b. Great Britain
    c. China
    d. Russia
    e. Nigeria

6. Which one of the following countries does not have a bicameral legislative system?
    a. Great Britain
    b. China
    c. Russia
    d. Nigeria
    e. Mexico

7. What are the three courts of the Court of Justice of the European Union?
    a. Court of Justice, the General Court, and the Civil Service Tribunal
    b. Supreme Court, Civil Court, and the Court of Appeals
    c. General Court, the Court of Appeals, and Civil Court
    d. District Court, the Court of Justice, and the Court of Appeals
    e. Court of Justice, the General Assembly, and the Court of Appeals.

8. The Iran Guardian Council of the Constitution has the power to veto laws that:
    a. Do not comply with the Constitution and popular opinion
    b. Do not comply with the Constitution and limit individual civil liberties
    c. Do not comply with the Constitution and encourage labor unrest
    d. Do not comply with the Constitution and Islam
    e. Do not comply with the Constitution and alienate the international community

9. Nigeria's economy has been petroleum based. Why has the diversification of the economy been slow?
    a. Border disputes
    b. Class struggles
    c. Corruption and mismanagement
    d. The effects of devaluation
    e. Environmental policies

10. What factored into the PRI party in Mexico losing the presidency in 2000?
    a. Foreign policies
    b. Collapse of longstanding labor unions
    c. Promises of education reform
    d. Regional cleavages
    e. The continued devaluation of the peso and the 1994 recession

11. Which political ideology believes in ending private ownership?
    a. Conservatism
    b. Socialism
    c. Communism
    d. Liberalism
    e. Fascism

12. Which two parties dominate Great Britain's House of Commons?
    a. Conservative and Labour
    b. Respect and Crossbench Peers
    c. Liberal Democrats and Labour
    d. Respect and Labour
    e. Conservative and Democratic Unionist Party

13. The socioeconomic status of which group of people was a contributing factor in the Chiapas Revolt?
    a. Those of Spanish descent
    b. Those of Mayan descent
    c. Descendants of the Aztecs
    d. Mestizos
    e. European immigrants

14. What two things legitimize authority and inspire unity?
    a. War and religion
    b. Nationalism and Socialist ideology
    c. Multistate structure and a dual party system
    d. Military authority and Communist ideology
    e. Religion and secular nationalism

15. Which country is an example of a Religious Nation-State?
    a. China
    b. Great Britain
    c. Iran
    d. Russia
    e. Mexico

16. Who has the power to appoint crucial positions and act as final arbiter in disputes between government branches in Iran?
    a. The Supreme Leader
    b. President
    c. Assembly of Experts
    d. Majles
    e. Council of Guardians

17. Which country could be called Occidental?
    a. Iran
    b. Russia
    c. Nigeria
    d. Great Britain
    e. China

18. What has Nigeria done to reform under the civilian government?
    a. Create biosafety legislation
    b. Privatize the government -owned petrochemical company
    c. Strong penalties concerning intellectual property rights
    d. Privatization of transportation
    e. Import inspection reforms

19. Weak organizational, financial, and political governments are at risk for:
    a. Insurgency
    b. Immigration
    c. Failed states
    d. Loss of military
    e. Centralists

20. A society with special interest groups focusing on the civil liberties that influence public policy is:
    a.   Socialist
    b. Communist
    c. Fascist
    d. Conservative
    e. Pluralist

21. Which country does not use a plurality voting system?
    a. Iran
    b. Great Britain
    c. China
    d. Mexico
    e. Nigeria

22. Nigeria is a member of which organization dedicated to promote "all fields of economic activity, particularly industry, transport, telecommunications, energy, agriculture, natural resources, commerce, monetary and financial questions, social and cultural matters…"?
    a. WTO
    b. ECOWAS
    c. EU
    d. SADC
    e. CEDEAO

23. What is a main difference between the formation of the Nigerian government and the government of Great Britain?
    a. Religious cleavages
    b. Political uprisings
    c. Economic cleavages
    d. Interstate war
    e. Immigration

24. What outside influence played a role in the Russian Revolution?
    a. Agrarian bureaucracy
    b. World War I
    c. Peasant grievances
    d. Modernization
    e. Land rights

25. _____ is a relatively new concept.
    a. State
    b. Government
    c. Sovereignty
    d. Emigration
    e. Nationalism

26. What is associated with a weak or failed state?
    a. Guaranteed employment
    b. Strong GDP
    c. Weak GDP
    d. Tariffs
    e. Immigration

27. What are three theories of comparative government?
    a. Cultural, structural, and rational-choice
    b. Behavioral, national, economic
    c. Structural, behavioral, modernization
    d. Economic, cultural, political
    e. National, behavioral, rational-choice

28. Members of the UN and the press have criticized China about which policy, and asked for change?
    a. Education
    b. Environmental
    c. Tax
    d. Monetary
    e. Organization

29. The United Nations Development Program (UNDP) is seeking to help Mexico establish:
    a. Gender equality
    b. Labor unions
    c. Environmental policy
    d. Religious tolerance
    e. Educational opportunities

30. The UN, EU, and ECOWAS are examples of _____ institutions.
    a. Regional
    b. Local
    c. Federal
    d. Supranational
    e. National

31. Which political party in Mexico does the Roman Catholic Church influence?
    a. PRI
    b. PAN
    c. PRD
    d. CTM
    e. INM

32. Iran is predominately a Muslim country. Which other religions are legally recognized?
    a. Christianity, Hinduism, and Buddhism
    b. Baha'i, Judaism, Hinduism, and Jainism
    c. Sunni Islam, Buddhism, and Sikhism
    d. Jainism, Hinduism, and Zoroastrianism
    e. Sunni Islam, Zoroastrianism, Judaism, and Christianity

33. Cleavages that overlap each other in certain areas such as class and ethnicity are_____:
    a. Crosscutting
    b. Reinforcing
    c. Stabilizing
    d. Coinciding
    e. Subordinating

34. What factors into democratization after an authoritarian regime such as post-Communism?
    a. Independent media
    b. Corporatism
    c. Socialism
    d. Devolution effects
    e. Tax increases

35. What was a contributing factor in the 1989 Student Movement and Tiananmen Square incident?
    a. Relaxed controls on literature
    b. International exchanges
    c. High inflation
    d. Political reforms
    e. Foreign investment

36. The Lords Spiritual and the Lords Temporal make up the _____.
    a. Council of Guardians
    b. House of Commons
    c. Assembly of Experts
    d. House of Lords
    e. Civil Service Tribunal

37. Which two countries made efforts to curb overpopulation in their countries in the late 20th century?
    a. Great Britain and Mexico
    b. Nigeria and China
    c. Iran and Great Britain
    d. Nigeria and Great Britain
    e. Great Britain and China

38. Which country has the problem of trying to unify 250 different ethnic groups?
    a. Nigeria
    b. China
    c. Great Britain
    d. Iran
    e. Mexico

39. Most political theorists, regardless of ideology, believe that _____ benefits all countries economically.
    a. Multistate structures
    b. Population control
    c. Free international trade
    d. Popular sovereignty
    e. Interest groups

40. What do remittances influence in Mexico?
    a. Taxation
    b. Devolution
    c. Social cleavages
    d. Major party dominance
    e. Migration

41. What two factors led to the revolution in Iran?
    a. Confusing policies and poorly trained officials
    b. Major party dominance and Westernization
    c. Inflation and weak oil production
    d. A widening gap between wealthy and poor and Westernization
    e. Military authority and Communist ideology

42. Which house does the Prime Minister of Great Britain sit in?
    a. House of Lords
    b. the Cabinet
    c. House of Commons
    d. Council of Guardians
    e. The Lords Spiritual

43. Which branch of the Russian government is having trouble transitioning to independence?
    a. The judicial
    b. The legislative
    c. The executive
    d. Special interest groups
    e. Political parties

44. Which of the following countries has a president and a prime minister?
    a. China
    b. Great Britain
    c. Mexico
    d. Iran
    e. Russia

45. Failed states are at greater risk for _____.
    a. Terrorist activity
    b. Special interest groups
    c. High taxation
    d. Population control
    e. Free international trade

46. The Chief Justice of the Supreme Court and the attorney general in Iran must be _____.
    a. Mestizos
    b. Mujtahids
    c. Shi'a
    d. Ijma'
    e. He jab

47. What type of system does China have?
    a. Dual-party
    b. Popular sovereignty
    c. Multi-party
    d. One-party
    e. Pluralist

48. Which military leader transitioned Nigeria to a civilian government?
    a. General Sani Abacha
    b. General Olusegun Obasango
    c. General Abdulsalami Abubakar
    d. General Olusegun Obasanjo
    e. General Shehu Shagari

49. How many European countries do not use the euro?
    a. one
    b. twelve
    c. five
    d. four
    e. three

50. Among the following, who is not a typical charismatic leader?
    a. Ayatollah Khomeini
    b. Winston Churchill
    c. Abdulsalami Abubakar
    d. Mao Tse Tung
    e. Vladamir Putin

Answers and Explanations

1. D: Although China claims executions have dropped recently, it is still thought to carry out more executions than the other choices. Pressure from human rights groups such as Amnesty International may be bringing the number down; however, the exact number of executions every year is a state secret. Sixty-eight crimes carry the death penalty, but currently only violent offenders are supposed to be executed and some lower court sentences are being rejected.

2. A: The EU is committed to the environment, humanitarian values, peace, stability, European solidarity, and a common market. The first two treaties shared a common theme. The Treaty of Paris, 1951, created a common steel and coal market between the original members. The Treaty of Rome, 1957, built the European Economic Community (EEC). These treaties both focused on creating a common market.

3. C: Although the 1993 Constitution ended limitations on absolute land ownership in Russia, implementation of the policy has been slow because land is viewed as a natural resource. Land ownership is only constitutionally guaranteed for three uses: housing and agriculture, industrial and commercial property, and construction.

4. E: The current Russian tax system is not very old. It is true that other countries are more experienced in collecting taxes, but the Russian government does not believe that to be the main cause of the poor tax revenue. Corruption, tax evasion, and lack of cooperation by local officials are considered the main problems. Russian tax rates are higher than in Western Europe; however, the government argues that the rates are comparable because so little tax money is actually collected.

5. B: A liberal democracy protects the constitutional rights of individuals. Representatives are elected by the people and their policies are tempered by existing constitutions. Even though Great Britain has no written constitution, historical documents, from the Magna Carta to Parliamentary law provide the foundation for the civil liberties of individuals. Great Britain focuses on individual civil liberties, making it a liberal democracy.

6. B: A bicameral legislature has more than one legislative house, such as an upper house and a lower house. This form of mixed government is supposed to ensure greater representation since it takes both houses to pass legislation. Many smaller countries or Communist regimes have unicameral legislature or one legislative house. Unicameral legislatures pass legislation more efficiently than bicameral legislation. China has a unicameral legislature, and Great Britain, Russia, Nigeria, and Mexico have bicameral legislatures.

7. A: There are three separate branches of the Court of Justice of the European Union. The Court of Justice identifies the accountability of administrations and national courts to apply EU laws. The General Court hears direct actions against EU employees, its members, community trademarks, and appeals against the Civil Service Tribunal. The Civil Service Tribunal handles matters between the EU and its civil servants.

8. D: The Iran Guardian Council of the Constitution is not part of the Judiciary, Legislature, or Executive branches. It is a separate political entity made up of six clerics and six jurists. They have veto power over laws passed by the parliament. Members interpret the constitution and determine whether or not a law is constitutional. They also have the right to veto laws that conflict with Islam.

9. C: Nigeria's economy has been petroleum based, but much of the revenue has been lost due to corrupt military regimes, mismanaged funds, and cost of implementing a democratic government. The military regimes failed to diversify. The GDP of Nigeria improved after 2007 because of the price of oil. Reforms on public-private infrastructure improvements such as roads and electricity are the current focus.

10. E: The PRI was Mexico's favored party throughout the twentieth century. In the late twentieth century, Mexico faced an ongoing economic crisis. After the peso was devalued in 1994, Mexico faced one of its worse recessions. Vicente Fox Quesada of the PAN party won the subsequent presidential election.

11. C: Socialism came out of the Industrial Revolution. Early Socialists believed that all people should be equal and the government should be responsible for ensuring equality. Karl Marx went further than many of his contemporaries by announcing the need to abolish all private ownership as well as the need for revolution. Although many early Communists considered themselves Socialists, completely ending private ownership was not embraced in Socialist ideology. Communist ideology embraced the end of private ownership, even if it has compromised the theory in practice.

12. A: The Labour Party began as a collection of   Socialist societies in the early twentieth century. The party split in 1981 and the Social Democratic Party was formed, but never gained a large following. Tony Blair led the "New Labor" in 1997 and 2001, taking a more moderate stance. The Conservative Party came from the Tory faction of the 17th century. Margaret Thatcher led the party in 1979, but her unpopularity reflected on the party. The decline of Tony Blair's popularity and infighting of the Labour Party has given Conservatives an edge in recent elections. There are more than two parties represented in the House of Commons. The Labour Party and the Conservative Party, however, dominate the electorate.

13. B: The Chiapas state was annexed as part of Mexico. Many people in this area are of Mayan descent, while the Mestizos of Spanish and Amerindian descent make up the majority in Mexico. This is one of the poorest states in Mexico and reforms did not make it to this area. A mainly agricultural community, the anti-poverty plan of President Salinas did not reach them. The people lived in poverty and felt they had nothing to lose by issuing the Declaration of the Lacandon Jungle.

14. E: Both religion and secular nationalism create a sense of community. They both influence worldviews and seek to manage chaos. Religion and nationalism have influenced the founding and formation of different governments throughout history.

15. C: The Islamic revolution in Iran united the country under the tenets of Islam. Islam influences the constitution of Iran and all policies, but there is a level of democracy in the electoral system. While religion has influenced the other countries listed, none of them are governed by specific religious beliefs.

16. A: The office of Supreme Leader is a lifelong position, and only the Assembly of Experts can remove him from power. He is the ultimate decision maker on all policy and has the right to remove the President from power. The Supreme Leader also appoints men to crucial positions and arbitrates disputes between government branches.

17. D: Occidentalism can be defined as the culture and characteristics of the West. This includes many countries in Western Europe and America. Russia is usually considered to be part of Eastern Europe, so it does not fall under Occidentalism category. Great Britain is considered to be part of western civilization.

18. B: Nigeria has privatized the only government-owned petrochemical company. The government also sold interests in other oil service companies. Biosafety legislation is still weak, as are the penalties concerning intellectual property rights. Corrupt inspections still present a problem in Nigeria, and the publically owned transportation system hinders the economic growth of the country.

19. A: Insurgency is a military struggle involving guerilla warfare of small rural bands. Insurgents can hold to different causes or ideologies. While it is commonly thought to be caused by ethnic or religious differences, weakened governments are more likely to see insurgency.

20. E: A pluralist society is made up of different special interest groups representing social minorities. These interest groups compete with each other to influence legislation. The power associated with these interest groups is always shifting.

21. C: A plurality voting system is one in which the winner is determined by the most votes, but not necessarily the majority of votes. It is used in single member districts. Every country listed except China uses a plurality voting system. China uses a parallel voting system.

22. B: Nigeria is a member of the Economic Community of West African States (ECOWAS). The ECOWAS is dedicated to "all fields of economic activity, particularly industry, transport, telecommunications, energy, agriculture, natural resources, commerce, monetary and financial questions, social and cultural matters… ." Fifteen countries are currently members of the ECOWAS.

23. D: Modern Nigeria was once a British colony that gained independence without war. Interstate war is a unifying factor in the formation of nations, and a key to effective taxation. This lack of conflict with neighboring countries is thought to be a reason for the slow development of Nigeria.

24. B: The Revolution of 1905 occurred for many of the same reasons as the 1917 Revolution. The Czar was able to end the rebellion using the military. Due to loans from western countries, Russia was included in World War I. The military involvement outside of Russia played a role in the success of the Revolution in 1917.

25. E: Different localities as a nation is a newer idea. Nations are united by societies once united under a local ruler or area, similar to a state. Nations unify under common interests, beliefs, ideologies or religion rather than locality. Nationalism unites people beyond the interest of their states.

26. C: The economic output of a country indicates its strength. Strong states typically have strong GDPs. Although not the only factor to consider, a weak GDP, especially when there is an abundance of natural resources, is a sign that the state is weak or failing.

27. A: While there is more than one method to studying comparative government, there are three classic theories. The cultural, structural, and rational-choice methods dominate comparative politics. Each one is "…embedded in strong research communities, scholarly traditions, and analytical languages." (Lichbach and Zuckerman: Research, Tradition, and Theory in Comparative Politics)

28. B: China has developed economically, but the cost to the environment is high. Environmental groups and the media constantly criticize high crop productions, deforestation, pollution, and energy use. The UN has pressured China to instill stricter environmental policies.

29. A: Although a general Act on Equality was adopted in 2006, women in many rural areas are still unaffected. Gender equality is an ongoing issue. The UNDP is allocating $1 million to the National Women's Agency (INM) for the promotion of gender equality and the prevention of violence against women.

30. D: Supranational institutions unite several states based on common interests. These institutions develop international laws. With the current globalization, different supranational institutions influence regulations on trade, human rights, and development.

31. B: The National Action Party (PAN) is similar to the Christian Democratic Party in Europe. The PAN is a more conservative party. Many of the restrictions placed on the Church in the 1917 Constitution were changed by the Salinas-led government (1991-1992).

32. E: Iran interprets the constitution through Shi'a Islam, which is the official religion of Iran. The minority religions of Sunni Islam, Zoroastrianism, Judaism, and Christianity are granted legal recognition and representation.

33. B: Crosscutting cleavages cut across cleavages and reduce the conflicts associated with social cleavages. Reinforcing cleavages, on the other hand, overlap each other and intensify conflicts and struggles. Ethnicity and class may or may not reinforce one another depending upon the circumstances.

34. A: Under authoritarian regimes, the media is closely regulated. Independent media informs citizens of government scandals, corruption, and unpopular policies. Access to new information and the views of more than one political party can have a profound impact on the views and actions of citizens. Independent media played an important role in the regions of the former USSR.

35. C: High inflation caused economic hardship for Chinese citizens. The death of reformer Hu Yaobang set the stage for a protest on a far-reaching scale. Intellectuals, students, and others congregated in Tiananmen Square in 1989. The government declared martial law and cleared the square by force June 3, 1989 and June 4, 1989.

36. D: The Lords Spiritual and Lords Temporal make up the House of Lords. The Archbishop of Canterbury and other Anglican leaders comprise the Lords Spiritual, and the Lords Temporal are hereditary or life peers. Life peers make up the majority in the House of Lords since legislation has limited the number of hereditary positions.

37. B: In an attempt to keep the population down, China instituted a one-child policy. Nigeria has the largest population in Africa. The government has provided more access to birth control and encouraged families to limit themselves to four children.

38. A: Regional and ethnic cleavages have been a political struggle for the government of Nigeria. Although English is the official language of Nigeria, the country is made up of a variety of languages and cultures. Religious influences also vary. Most citizens align themselves with Muslim, Christian, and indigenous African beliefs.

39. C: While many Communist regimes limit international trade, liberals, Marxists, social democrats, and conservatives support the idea of free international trade. Mercantilists do not support free international trade, but mercantilism is not a widely respected ideology.

40. E: Remittances are funds that migrant workers in other countries, such as the United States, send back to their families in Mexico. Remittances are an important source of income for the economy. The dependence of families on remittances influences migration trends. Migration to the U.S. from Mexico has decreased with the slowing economy and stricter immigrations laws.

41. D: Iran's resources were strained in 1973. Despite growing oil revenue, inflation caused the gap between the rich and poor to grow. Many traditionalists felt that the number of foreign visitors and increasing Western influence threatened the culture of Iran. Both of these factors contributed to the revolution.

42. C: Great Britain's Prime Minister receives political authority from the House of Common's voters. The Prime Minister has the authority to appoint and dismiss ministers. Recent customs have the Prime Minister always sitting with the House of Commons.

43. A: Russia's judicial system has seen many reforms and is similar to the judicial system of other democracies. Many judges, however, still see themselves as government employees who need to serve the best interests of the state.

44. E: The Russian government has a president and prime minister, a system set up after the fall of the Soviet Union. The current Russian prime minister is Vladimir Putin, and the president is Dmitry Medvedev, who succeeded Putin as president.

45. A: Failed states are financially weak. They have greater corruption, internal conflict, and little equality. These conditions combined with weak government control do little to limit terrorist activity. A failed state can become a threat to the international community.

46. B: Iran operates under Muslim law. Mujtahids are trained jurists who are deemed qualified to interpret the law. Other justices and the faqih appoint the Chief Justice. The Attorney General is also the State Prosecutor. Both of these men serve as part of the High Council of Justice for five-year terms.

47. D: China has a one-party system. Although there are citizens who might not identify with the Communist Party of China (CPC), the CPC still dominates. The country has eight minor parties, but all of them are under the supervision of the Communist Party. China has made recent reforms, but changing the one-party system is not one of them.

48. C: General Abdulsalami Abubakar took over the government after the death of General Sani Abacha. When General Sani Abacha ruled, Nigeria suffered from human rights violations, corruption, and international distress. General Abdulsalami Abubakar came to power in 1998, and he transitioned Nigeria to a civilian government in 1999.

49. E: Great Britain has opposed the euro, but it is not the only country to do so. Denmark and Sweden have also refused to adopt the currency. Nine territories in the EU do not use the euro. Currently, 12 countries use the euro: Belgium, Germany, Greece, Spain, France, Ireland, Italy, Luxembourg, The Netherlands, Austria, Portugal, and Finland.

50. C: General Abdulsalami Abubakar is not generally considered to be a charismatic leader. The leadership of Nigeria was given to him when he, reportedly, did not want it. Abubakar did not have the trust of the people when he took power; he had to solve problems and earn trust by eventually transitioning to a civilian government.

Made in the USA
Middletown, DE
27 February 2016